BINGE

BINGE

BINGE

TYLER OAKLEY

SIMON & SCHUSTER

First published in Great Britain in 2015 by Simon & Schuster UK Ltd
1st Floor, 222 Gray's Inn Road, London, WC1X 8HB

A CBS company

Originally published by Gallery Books, an imprint of
Simon & Schuster, New York

Manufactured in Italy

1 3 5 7 9 10 8 6 4 2

A CIP catalogue for this book is available from the British Library

Interior design by Jane Archer (www.psbella.com)

ISBN 978-1-4711-4513-1
ISBN 978-1-4711-4590-2 (limited signed edition)
ISBN 978-1-4711-4514-8 (ebook)

NOTE TO READERS: Some names
and identifying details have been changed.

For my people.

contents

introduction

G O AHEAD, BINGE.
I'm not saying go out and snort a bunch of cocaine or do anything that's going to seriously put you or the people around you in danger, obviously.

Binge on the things that bring fulfillment and happiness and satisfaction and make you feel alive. Binge on people who fascinate you and love that wakes you up from monotony. Binge on exploring, both your hometown and the farthest continent. Binge on the time you spend bettering yourself and petting dogs. Binge on picking your grandma's brain and learning the story of the time she got catfished. Binge on giving, in all senses. Binge on indulging.

We're told every day from an early age that moderation is key. Count your calories, wait a while before you tell someone you love them, and remember that balance is the path to happiness. While all of those are great in theory, does a lesson taught from someone else's mistakes resonate just as deeply as the ones you learn yourself? When you binge, you find your own boundaries.

Even if I spend every waking moment attempting to keep my life in balance, I'm going to fuck up. Having already fucked up quite a few times in my life, and having lived to tell the tale, I don't regret any of it.

I've binged plenty of times in my life, sometimes for better, sometimes for worse. Regardless, I indulged. This collection is the result.

mathew

TYLER OAKLEY ISN'T MY REAL NAME. *Ahh!* See? This book is full of surprises! Right off the bat, *bam!* You've got an exclusive! Truth be told, my real name is Mathew Tyler Oakley, but it feels like I've always gone by Tyler. Back in kindergarten, another Mathew was in my class, and that simply would not do. I was not there to leave it up to my classmates to label the two Mathews with adjectives—because Lord knows I would have been "chubby Mathew," which was not the branding I was going for at age five (or ever).

So, I came home one day and told my parents that I'd be going by Tyler. I needed to be one of a kind at school if I wanted to make any impression. I mean, imagine two celebrities sharing a name! How confusing and ridiculous would that be? Well, just look at Michelle Williams. No, not the one who was in *Brokeback Mountain* or *Blue Valentine* or *My Week with Marilyn* . . . the one who used to be in Destiny's

Child with Beyoncé. *See?!* This kind of confusion was *not* something I wanted to deal with down the line.

So here I am, as what has almost become two separate people, Mathew Tyler Oakley and Tyler Oakley. As time has gone on, Mathew has become my more private identity—someone who I very much protect. Tyler is who I generously offer, at school, in life, and on YouTube. Mathew is what my parents and siblings call me, and the name I sign my binding contracts with, and Tyler is who makes embarrassing challenge videos and meets guys on Grindr. I've always been both, and to some people I'm more one than the other.

And now you know. But for me to give you Mathew right off the bat . . . that's me trusting you. It's me saying hi, welcome to my life, not everything is pretty or perfect or edited with jump cuts. That's Tyler. You know Tyler. It's time for me to tell you all of Mathew's stories.

But still call me Tyler because, honestly, do I even *look* like a Mathew at this point? Yeah, no.

march 22

T HOUGH I HAVE NO RECOLLECTION OF IT, I think I can safely assume my first birthday was spectacular. I probably ate the fuck out of some cake, and I probably shit my pants. I assume that I'll be spending my very last birthday the exact same way, not to mention a few in between if things go unexpectedly well.

Having birthday parties has always been an inexhaustible source of stress for me. What happens if you plan an extravagant celebration for yourself and no one shows up? Or what if someone plans a surprise party for you? Like, what if you're rushing home to shit explosively, you burst through the front door, and—*Surprise!*—in more ways than one? My mom often recounted the story of her own worst birthday—a surprise party her best friend attempted to throw for her, which nobody attended except the two of them. The horror of that story stuck with me, and each March 22, I take a firm stance against expectations.

Then there's the issue of attending other people's birthday

parties. I once attended a birthday-party horror story like my mom's. Karen was in the grade above me; she was a bit of a loner who lacked social skills, and she had a severe crush on me. Although I obviously didn't reciprocate the feelings (because of the gay), I attended her party with my (hot, straight) best friend, Dolan. Her dad welcomed us into their home and directed us downstairs, and as we descended into her basement, we found her alone, pacing. We made some small talk, but soon realized you can't mingle if you're the only ones at the party. How were we going to escape?

My typical go-to move while attending any social function is what I've heard referred to as the Irish exit—where you slip out of the party, unnoticed, without saying good-bye to anyone. Good-byes are messy and an unnecessary disruption to the flow of an event, and honestly, what if you don't want to hug certain people? If I could Irish-exit out of every life situation, I would. Meetings, funerals, sexual encounters—that's my preference. Unfortunately, there would be no Irish exits out of this particular soiree.

Just when I thought things couldn't get more uncomfortable, the birthday girl suggested a game of Twister. I glanced at Dolan and realized things were about to get delightfully homoerotic. Karen spun the dial of the Twister board and watched as Dolan and I stretched and rubbed against each other. It seemed a bit voyeuristic for her, and the homosexual undertones far outweighed the awkward silences between each spin (at least for me). In what I'd later describe as my favorite moment of the evening, Dolan collapsed on me, and before any other games could be suggested, Karen's mom invited us upstairs for cake. As Dolan and I decided it might be time to call it a night (at 4:00 p.m.), Karen's dad offered to show us his VHS collection "real quick." A thirty-minute tour through his wall-to-wall, floor-to-ceiling VHS tape collection followed. It felt like an episode of *Hoarders* come to life, but unfortunately no piles of garbage collapsed on me to put me out of my misery.

Maybe even worse for me than not having anyone show up to a birthday party is receiving a birthday gift I don't like. I realize all gifts deserve gratitude, but as someone who generally doesn't need much, I've developed a fair amount of stress over opening presents in front of people. This is quite possibly the grossest first-world problem in history, but don't act like you haven't been there. I'd always suggest to my parents that I open my presents in the privacy of my own room, but they would have none of that. This resulted in a lot of overselling on my part. *I've always wanted a novelty oversize TV remote from the dollar store! Thank you, you really get me!*

For my tenth birthday, I decided to take matters into my own hands. Coincidentally, this was the year that I decided that it was finally time to become cool. I did a bit of research on the playground to figure out what all my hip peers were into, and I found that, overwhelmingly, everyone loved yo-yos. After handing out my birthday invitations to every boy in my class, I discreetly let it be known that if anyone was in need of a gift idea, I was in the market for a new yo-yo. On the day of my party, all thirteen boys showed up with gift bags about the same weight and size, overflowing with tissue paper, and I knew I was poised to be the next "coolest kid in school." As I opened the bags, I feigned surprise at each and every yo-yo, but my mom was far from convinced.

"You don't even know how to use a yo-yo!" My mom, Jackie, exclaimed while cutting the cake, exposing me as a fraud in front of all of my fifth-grade friends. "You surely don't need thirteen of them!" she continued, handing out paper plates of cake and melting ice cream. I had just gone from yo-yo prodigy, connoisseur, and collector to yo-yo pretender whose *mother* didn't *allow* coolness. The next day, she made me return each and every yo-yo to the kiosk in the mall. A greedy ascent followed by an unspooling free fall; like the yo-yo itself, so went my social status.

Next, there's the trouble of wanting to get invited to certain birthday parties, but not being cool enough to be considered. In elementary school, I was awkward and a loser, and when I got an invite to Andrew McGonigle's ninth birthday party, I was beside myself. As far as I was concerned—and I very much was—Andrew was the most popular kid and biggest trendsetter at Dibble Elementary School. He once checked out *The Giving Tree* from the school's library, and the next thing you know, every Shel Silverstein book was on the school's waiting list. He decided Backstreet Boys were better than *NSYNC, and all the girls and the gays threw away their Lance Bass dolls. (Sorry, Lance). He single-handedly made WWJD bracelets a fashion staple. But never mind Jesus: Dibble Elementary had to know, WWAMD? No matter what his choices were, the entire school trusted his judgment and taste. This was someone I spent years trying to impress. Getting an invite to his birthday? Looks like I had finally done something right!

Andrew's birthday invite said to bring a winter coat, as we'd be riding his four-wheelers (so butch—I was in love) around his backyard. Knowing how safety-conscious my parents were, I tried everything to distract them from reading the invitation's fine print, to no avail. They called ahead to let Mrs. McGonigle know that during the four-wheeling portion of the party, I was to wait inside like a sickly child on a snow day. So, while the cool kids took turns spinning out in Andrew's muddy backyard, I watched from the kitchen window, forlorn. It was the last time I was invited to one of Andrew McGonigle's birthday parties.

In fifth grade, a kid in my class named Donny had a birthday approaching. Oh, and he was a Wiccan, did I mention that? The guest list was exclusive, as he was planning a movie theater excursion, and a limited number of tickets had already been purchased. During the weeks leading up to his birthday, Donny became drunk with power. For the smallest infractions, he breezily disinvited guests and redistributed their tickets accordingly. I was already terrified to cross him, fearing a Wiccan hex or curse. Now, with the added threat of being exiled from free popcorn and the new Disney film, *Dinosaur*, it was like I was walking on eggshells. When we played four square during recess, I'd lightly lob the ball in his direction. I'd share all my Warheads candy with him. I even started to hide my Andrew McGonigle-inspired WWJD bracelet around him, just in case our conflicting faiths would set him off. After those two weeks of treading delicately, I made the final cut and was able to attend. Unfortunately, *Dinosaur* sucked, which Donny's clairvoyance spells hadn't foreseen. That day, I decided that going forward, no birthday party is worth that level of stress just to get an invite.

While I was growing up, the most frightening birthday parties were the ones hosted at Chuck E. Cheese. If you're unfamiliar, Chuck E. Cheese is a fictional, human-size mouse who owns a pizza arcade. Chuck is part of a band called Munch's Make Believe Band, which performs animatronically at the front of the dining area. The band is what nightmares are made of.

The robotic band jerks to and fro murderously, as they perform deceptively innocent songs akin to Kidz Bop. My mind can't help but imagine the lights going dim and their nearly depleted batteries producing low, slowed-down, demonic versions of their songs in the dark—an image that terrifies me even to this day. Luckily, nowadays I'm old enough to buy the two beers the restaurant permits each adult to purchase, and my fear of Munch's Make Believe Band is blunted by alcohol.

In middle school, birthdays became all about party games, or, should I say, *game*: spin the bottle. Even though I had a few girlfriends throughout my middle-school years, I was far from wanting to make out with them, and if I ever did, it was with boys in mind. At parties, we'd assemble ourselves in a circle in whoever's basement and awkwardly take turns spinning an empty Aquafina bottle, then slowly leaning forward to peck each other on the lips. I was alive with the possibility of the bottle's landing on another guy. To this day, I can't drink from a bottle without the impulse to leverage it into making out with strangers. Maybe at my next birthday. Zayn Malik, Zac Efron, Nick Jonas, Darren Criss . . . save the date, you're all invited.

Since 2008, my birthday has coincided with Playlist Live, a Florida-based convention with thousands of screaming tweens hoping to meet their favorite YouTubers. I didn't have much of an audience when I first started to attend conventions, so the occasional "Happy birthday!" as I wandered through the convention center was a nice surprise.

My channel grew a bit more every year, as did the opportunities offered to me during conventions. From getting a chance to speak on panels and being interviewed onstage to receiving an invite as a guest, I felt like I was actually becoming a YouTuber. Every year, more and more people began to come up to me to wish me a happy birthday. At Disneyland, there's a pin you can wear on your birthday, and if any cast members see you wearing it, they have to go out of their way to wish you a happy birthday. That's what Playlist Live began to feel like, but without a hot Aladdin being required by company policy to chat me up.

My birthdays at YouTube conventions gave me so many first encounters with creators I respect so much: Zoe Sugg, Hannah Hart, Grace Helbig, GloZell, Mamrie Hart, and Troye Sivan, to name just a few. These were by far the best gifts I could ever have asked for.

This year, with Playlist Live happening a month early, my birthday weekend was free, and I had two options: fear the possibility of what could go wrong and just not celebrate, or take a chance and live it up. So I rented out a roller rink, bought out an entire wig store, and threw the biggest drunk, roller-skating, wig birthday extravaganza the world has ever seen. The older I get, the more I realize what a gift a true friend is. Especially since my mom can't make me return those.

dial-up delight

M Y CARNAL THIRST HAS ALWAYS BEEN unquenchable, but when I was growing up, it was out of control—and with no cute boys ready and willing at my disposal, I turned to man's *other* best friend: porn.

I vividly remember my first glimpse of adult content. I was in my single digits, at my Grandma Oakley's place—a shabby trailer home occupied by my grandma, my uncle, my older cousin, and their dog, Peanut. My cousin was in either a goth or a Juggalo phase; my uncle had a mustache and often asked family members to pull his finger whenever he had to fart; Peanut was a balding poodle; and my grandma spent all day on her new computer sending e-cards to distant relatives. You can't pick your family—but if I could, I'd still pick this motley crew.

The day I saw the first erect penis that wasn't attached to me, I was wasting time playing *Battletoads* on Nintendo with my cousin. In between levels, he looked at me and asked the question that turns every boy into a man: "Wanna see some boobs?" My time had come.

He closed the doorway beads that separated his carpeted room from the linoleum kitchen, to give us a little more privacy. Quietly, he fished out a magazine from the laundry basket. Sitting on the edge of his bed, we opened up this holy scripture, and I sat in awe. In between pages of articles and advertisements, I saw it all—big-breasted women in lace outfits, spread-eagled and grinning. We flipped through the pages in silence until one particular picture, small and in the corner, caught my eye.

There she was, a literal goddess—naked, poised, and perfect. The picture was taken from above, she was on her back, just her face showing, making smoldering eye contact with the camera. Her entire aura communicated one clear and unified message to eight-year-old Tyler Oakley: envy me, you closeted, little gay boy languishing in small-town Michigan—for I have everything you could ever desire.

It was undeniably true, she had it all. I most admired this woman not due to her flawless complexion or flowing hair, though both looked amazing—but because she had literally a dozen dicks coming at her from every angle. It was as though she were beset by a school of inquisitive lampreys. (Google it, I once had to dissect one.) If that's too horrifying, you could imagine she was the baby sun in *Teletubbies*, but her normally luminous rays were now engorged and veiny. Now don't get me wrong, I don't normally measure a woman's worth by the number of erections currently on her face. That said, I can't pretend I wasn't jealous.

I gawked at the picture of the unforgivably selfish dick hoarder, and I held firm to the pages while my cousin tried to flip to the next. She was in heaven, and I was high on just her fumes. I knew, then and there, with the *Battletoads* music droning in the background, what my dreams were for this life and who I was meant to be.

With an abrupt clattering, the door beads divided and my grandma shuffled in—as both of us scrambled to hide the goods. Grandma Oakley knew what was up, demanded the contraband, and began screaming in exasperation. I sat, dazed, thinking about the ineffable, otherworldly Goddess of Dick. I could not unsee what I had seen. My time with the magazine may have been short, but it left a permanent impression: I needed to see more penis.

Another pre-Internet porn experience was during a family visit to Canada. Side note: when I was younger, Canada was the most mythical place in the world to me because they sold milk in bags instead of jugs or cartons. Seriously, so fucked up. Anyway, back to porn. I was visiting family and friends, and having a slumber party with one of their kids. He was impossibly cool—he skateboarded and downloaded music illegally with Napster. I was in awe of how much of a badass he was.

For some reason, I thought I could impress him by claiming that I had the power to tell if a girl was a slut. To call my bluff, he busted out a *Hustler* magazine filled with solo shots of dozens of girls. He then made me go page by page, labeling each girl as either a slut or not a slut—for what felt like hundreds of pages. My heart was pounding because I was sure that this page-by-page test would not only prove my claim false, but also expose me as *gay*. By the end of it, he got bored and went back to playing *Tony Hawk's Pro Skater*, and I was left exhausted and shaken. That day, I learned that with slut-shaming comes instant karma.

Back then, we didn't have fiber-optic or even cable Internet. Dial-up Internet was the norm—and for those who don't know what that was, it was a fucking mess: you used your landline (which apparently nobody even has nowadays) and a modem. While you were online, nobody could use the phone. Not very discreet for private browsing, and far from fast—so video clips were out of the question. If you wanted to see dick, you literally searched *penis*, and that was about as good as it got. Thus, I discovered erotic fiction.

I found a website with tons of stories, ranging from embellished nonfiction to outright fantasy, detailing sexcapades with words like *throbbing* and *turgid*, in which every person was six feet three inches, muscular, and blessed with a chiseled jaw. You could sort by tons of categories such as "college" and "athletic," and I let my mind run wild. All stories were user submitted, and at the age of twelve, I felt accomplished enough in my English classes to submit my own fantasy. So I guess this book is technically my second time getting published. I don't remember all of the details about the fictional story I wrote, but I do remember it had to do with a hot guy I knew in middle school coming over after school for an intimate tutoring session.

I remember the one story I read repeatedly growing up was called something along the lines of "Fratguys Whip Out a Ruler." It was a tale for a simpler time, chronicling four college bros who wrestle in their dorm room until they get understandably curious about who is packing the most heat. One of their names was Blake, and ever since I've longed for a Blake of my own. After reading that masterpiece, twelve-year-old Tyler Oakley began furiously studying for the ACT and was *getting accepted to college no matter the cost.*

Even though I had only limited hours to use the dial-up Internet, I managed to save dozens of stories to my computer, expertly disguised as homework files—easily accessible, yet undetectable. Mom and Dad, if you ever saw me working on something labeled "Science Essay"—now you know, sorry.

When my Internet connection got a bit better, I moved on to browsing official porn websites. I'd go hog wild and click on everything, something I didn't realize would come back to haunt me. One day, I was hanging out in the office while my mom was on the computer and, out of nowhere, *screams* from the desk chair. I jolted in her direction, horrified to see a pop-up ad flashing a huge, veiny dick wiggling all over the screen, jumping from corner to corner, impossible to close amid my mom's shrieks. Worse, my brother ran into the room, cackling, as my mom frantically attempted to shield us from the oversize meat tube terrorizing our peaceful home. *"Why is this happening to us?!"*

As a last resort, my mom frantically unplugged the computer. I hurriedly assured her that *viruses* and *hackers* plagued the Internet, *thriving* off the *havoc* they wreak on wholesome families like *ours*. They *live* to force pop-up ads on us, the *dirtier* the *better*. She sighed and at least acted as if she believed me, but my flustered demeanor and flop sweat must have been obvious and telling: that veiny monster was all my fault, and we all knew it.

Years later, I now have fast Internet and know how to delete my browsing history—but something was thrilling about the days of spending hours of my time online, downloading one fifteen-second clip and never knowing whether I would be able to get rid of the virus it left on our computer. Nowadays, your private sexual perversions are safe and sound, known only by you and, well, the government. Sigh, we had it so good back then, and we didn't even know it.

fecal matters

OVER MY LIFETIME, I've had an interesting relationship with poop. Yes, this is becoming one of *those* chapters before it even really gets started.

The rectum is a grand thing. My favorite thing about the human body is that we're all basically doughnuts. The gastrointestinal tract starts with the mouth, goes on a funky journey through the esophagus, stomach, small and large intestines, and rectum, with the grand finale (like most grand finales) at the anus. The gastrointestinal tract is the human body's doughnut hole, a tube within a tube. I don't know about you, but I consider my body's ability to shit to be an actual superpower. The path from your mouth to your anus is proof of intelligent design.

I'd be the definition of class, if the definition of class were as follows:

---

class [klas, klahs] *n 1. a person who nicknames the assholes of others*

Yes, the rumors are true. If you're one of my friends, I've probably nicknamed your anus. It's not like I spend my time thinking about your butthole, but it's one of those things where, like . . . you know how pet owners look like their dogs? Listen, I know you know what I'm talking about, stop *looking* at me. Though now that I'm trying to explain myself, I feel incredibly uncomfortable. Listen, your asshole is precious. It deserves to be shown love, and that's all I'm doing. *Let me live. Let your* asshole *live.*

Korey Kuhl is one of my absolute favorite humans and one of the funniest people I've ever met. We've known each other since the exact day I created my YouTube channel back in 2007, and we have been besties since. Nowadays, we cohost a podcast called *Psychobabble*, and he helps me keep my life in order in every way possible. Over the course of our friendship, we've compiled a solid list of nicknames for many of our friends' back doors. If you need inspiration for nicknaming an asshole in your life, here are some that we've given sphincters over the years. Please take your time and allow each one to blossom fully in your mind:

cousin it	bermuda triangle
junk drawer	third eye blind
miss piggy	hidden valley
charlotte's web	boxtroll
black hole	krustyland
chamber of secrets	google hangout
boingo hotspot	bloomin' onion

This list may be the most valuable thing I've ever written. Let this chapter be my legacy. If you come up with any incredible nicknames for assholes, let me know on Twitter right now by tweeting me: @tyleroakley. Thanks in advance.

I wouldn't call myself a particularly stingy person, but while I was growing up, my shit was not to be parted with. It's become one of those stories my parents and siblings think are hilarious to bring up in front of friends and boyfriends, which is probably why I'm left with neither after any visit to my home in Michigan. According to family legend, I was an episode of *Hoarders* when it came to my poop, and I refused to defecate, even if it meant I'd pass out from holding it in. I'd hide in closets, twisting my legs and clenching as hard as I could until it was no longer possible, then finally release my gift to this vale of tears. It was as if I had a personal vendetta against our home's plumbing system.

Because I probably can't get away with showing an actual image of my poop in this book, please enjoy the next best thing, what is probably closest in similarity: the image of Banana, the seven-foot albino python, who accompanied Ms. Britney Spears in her 2001 MTV Video Music Awards performance of "I'm a Slave 4 U." Actually, we don't have the rights. Just go find the video on the Internet. There, now you know.

My refusal to shit for days on end became my thing. Which, if you're going to have a thing, is not the one you want. This quirk also created my completely rational fear of clogging toilets. When I unleashed my tsunami, or *poo-nami*, if you will, I found my foxhole religion. I'd bargain out loud with a

God whose existence I normally doubted, in exchange for an incident-free flush of the toilet. As I pushed down the lever, I stood before the great white porcelain throne, ready to receive judgment. More often than not, God was wrathful, and it came to pass that the water of the toilet prevailed upward and increased greatly, as I scrambled around in a mad panic. I've faced many a flooded bathroom in my day, and I wouldn't wish it on an enemy.

When I was in elementary school, my anxiety over shitting in public—due to the probability of clogging a toilet—led to me doing something far worse. I became known in the principal's office as the boy who shit himself all the time. My parents would stock up on underwear and leave half of my supply at the secretary's desk. If I entered the main office sheepishly, I needn't explain. My reputation, like my stench, preceded me. At one point during this phase of my life (I swear it's over now), I think I was getting a little *too* comfortable with the availability of clean undies in the office. On one normal day of shitting myself on the playground, I politely excused myself from my friends at the swings and made my way inside. As I confidently strutted in to casually collect a fresh pair of unmentionables, the secretary looked at me as if I were shit out of luck. My stomach dropped when she told me I was all out of clean underwear. I froze, unable to speak. Thankfully, my scent did all of my talking, and she pulled out the lost-and-found box from underneath the desk. She rummaged around and eventually found some Barbie-themed pink panties. She looked at me doubtfully, but I was in no position to bargain. I haven't worn women's underwear since, but I do feel that if I ever attempt drag, the roots run deep.

Eventually, I cleaned up my act and stopped shitting myself (at least until college, we'll get to that) and began to poop on a regular schedule. But to this day, clogging a toilet is my biggest fear—because just when you think a clogged toilet is terrifying, it could always be worse. It could be overflowing. You could be at a friend's house. It could also be during dinner, and the bathroom is right next to the dining room. There could also be someone knocking on the door. They could also not have a plunger in the bathroom. It could also have been diarrhea. How would that clog, you might ask? Enough of anything will clog a toilet. Sound far-fetched? I've been in *all* of these hells, and I never want to go back.

When you have siblings, you wish the best for them. You also want to protect them, especially when they're different. When I discovered my little brother had a superpower, I felt excitement, astonishment, but, above all, fear that he would not be accepted by society.

My little brother Connor was just a toddler, being potty trained. I was in my room, minding my own business, when out of the blue I heard him screaming my name from down the hall. I rushed to see if he was okay, and I found him in the bathroom.

"What is wrong?!" I croaked, fearing for his life.

"Look what I did!" he said proudly, pointing at the toilet.

I stepped into the bathroom, slowly, and peered into the toilet bowl. There, sunk to the very bottom of the water, sat a perfectly spherical poop. It was as smooth as a garden gazing ball. Peering into it, I lost myself, as the perfection of its shape couldn't be replicated by any artisan. I looked back at my brother where he stood, arms akimbo, grinning from ear to ear. To this day, I don't know how he did it, or if he ever was able to duplicate this magnificent feat—but I'll always recall that day as the one on which Connor revealed his first glimpse of extraordinary talent.

In some respects, I commend my parents for making me so self-sufficient when I was younger. I made my own school lunches, I organized my own car pools, I gave myself the talk on the birds and the bees—all while still in the single digits. I was becoming an independent seven-year-old, and all of my training felt like the preparation needed to become a real-life Macaulay Culkin in *Home Alone*.

Despite my best efforts, not everything went smoothly. My worst mishap had to be when I attempted to do my own laundry in elementary school. I thought I had done everything right—I sorted my darks and lights, my delicates and my denim, cleaned out the filters, measured detergents just so, but something out of my control went wrong, and the results were dire. As I descended into the basement after my first load had washed for an hour, I was immediately repulsed by a foul smell and prayed to God it was just one of the dogs having shit on the carpet. Not until I reached the end of my descent did I realize I was in too deep.

My sock was instantly freezing wet, and the smell was overwhelming. I looked down and saw a murky liquid flooding the basement, then groaned as I quickly made my way over to the washer. In a moment, I swung the top of the washer open to find it was filled to the brim with sewage. *My delicates!* I probably screamed. Shit was literally everywhere, and my clothes were in a stew of filth.

I'm not sure how this story ends. I don't remember how I got myself out of this. Writing now, it appears I may have blacked out and woken up in third grade. I don't remember much else from being seven years old. All I know now is that I'd rather take my dirty clothes to the fluff-and-fold Laundromat down the street than attempt to do my own laundry. It's not that I can't, it's just that I'd rather be safe than shitty.

ladies' man

WHEN I WAS IN ELEMENTARY SCHOOL, my older sister had a best friend named Stacia. She was blond and had a raspy voice, and for some reason I was crushing hard. I was a long way from figuring out my sexual orientation, and it seemed like the thing to do. She was constantly over at our house, and I'd find any excuse to butt my way into their playdates, but I soon realized a girl in fourth grade had no interest in a boy in second grade. Older women, ya feel?

One night when my sister had Stacia over, I decided it was time for me to make my move. It was dinnertime, and my mom had prepared a special meal of several courses of canned foods. One dish stood out to me as the key to Stacia's heart. I asked my mom to please pass the canned peach halves. I scooped a few onto my plate and looked up to make sure Stacia was paying attention. If this didn't capture her heart, nothing would.

With my fork, I picked up an entire peach half, put it into my mouth, and attempted to swallow it whole. As soon as it entered my throat, I began to choke, and my face turned a deep purple as I gagged and heaved. Pandemonium overtook the dinner table, my sister laughed, and Stacia looked on in horror. My mom screamed, jumping out of her seat and making her way toward me, wrapping her arms around my rotund body and pumping it an attempted Heimlich maneuver. (Until my early twenties, I thought it was called the Heimlich remover. Which makes more sense, if you think about it.)

With one final pump to my chest, the half peach flew out of my mouth and landed in the middle of the table full of food. Coughing and dripping sweat, I looked up at Stacia, who sat completely still, mortified. My sister rolled her eyes, took Stacia by the hand, and fled the dinner table. Interestingly enough, two decades later, I'm still gagging during my go-to attempt to demonstrate affection.

In fourth grade, I moved on from Stacia to Kayla Butterfield. She was the prettiest girl in my class. Because Andrew McGonigle, the coolest kid in school, liked her, I too had to act like she was my one and only. I wasn't effortlessly cool like Andrew, nor was I the star of the soccer team like Andrew, but I had recently discovered one thing I had that he lacked: nearsightedness. With this diagnosis came a pair of brand-new glasses, bright purple and blue, with *Blurple* written in Comic Sans on the side.

My Blurple glasses set me apart, and I was ready to use them to win over Kayla's affections. One day while on the playground, I decided it was now or never and walked up to Kayla and her friends.

"Hey, ladies," I said suavely, attempting to be nonchalant

and cool, like Danny Zuko, if Danny Zuko were to tuck a T-shirt
into some pleated khakis.

"Hi, Tyler," said Courtney, one of Kayla's friends.

"So . . . uhhh . . ." I had already run out of things to say, and
I was quickly panicking. *Abort mission,* said my mind. But my
heart said, *Use your glasses.*

"Look what my glasses can do," I said nervously, taking off
my spectacles. I began to bend the stems back and forth, twisting the frames to and fro by the bridge between the two lenses.
When the girls folded their arms, unimpressed, I hastened the

speed of my maneuver, until suddenly my glasses snapped in two. I gasped and the girls snorted, not even attempting to conceal their contempt. My eyes widened and my jaw dropped. I looked up from my broken glasses to my crush, who was laughing at my expense. Her silhouette was blurry without my corrective lenses, but her feelings for me were crystal clear.

The rest of my day was spent with tape holding the two halves of my glasses together, and knowing me, I probably also shit myself during recess. Not even a Scholastic Book Fair or a Lunchables could have turned my day around—and so I decided to give up hope on ever falling in love with Kayla Butterfield.

The farthest I ever got with a girl was when I was eleven and obsessed with an online video game in which people from all over the world could interact with each other in real time. In the game, the two of us met during a quest, when I was stuck in a corner of a dungeon and couldn't escape. She healed me from afar and saved me from dying. It was love at first fight. We then coordinated our time spent playing the game so that we could adventure together and explore the world, and eventually we went on a quest that culminated with our getting married in-game. Clearly I respect the sanctity of marriage: the union of one swashbuckler and one mage.

When I was twelve, I moved off to a new school district, and I was ready to reinvent myself. Sure I was still pudgy with questionable style, but now I was in a new town where nobody knew I had a long history of shitting myself. New year, new underwear, new me!

Enter: Andrea Lochner. She was cute and taller than me and had a full mouth of aggressive-looking braces. One morning on the school bus, she told me she liked me, and from that point on I guess we were dating. I feel bad admitting now that I wasn't into her, mostly because she was sweet and bought me a stuffed animal for Valentine's Day. The problem was . . . I was just then admitting to myself that I was totally gay and that she was totally not a guy. I mustered up the courage to break up with her, and we went our separate ways.

Ten years later, while I was innocently pole-dancing at a seedy gay bar in Michigan, I bumped into Andrea. I screamed over the loud music that I wanted to introduce her to my boyfriend, and she yelled back that she wanted to introduce me to her girlfriend. Funny how all things work out, if you just give them a decade.

binge

I WAS ALWAYS A BIT PLUMP. My chubby cheeks didn't complement my short stature, and the bowl haircut topping it all off wasn't helping. My personal life was flopping hard, and between custody hearings to decide which family I was going to live with, moving cities, completely starting over in a new school district, realizing I was gay (but also unable to tell anyone), and my family's being poorer than ever before, I was a bit stressed for twelve years old.

For years, therapists would tell me that I coped with my anxieties by warping my relationship with food. They said that while I felt I had no say in the ups and downs I was going through, I could at least control my relationship with food—that is, until I lost all control. I'm still figuring out the how and the why of everything that happened, even a decade later, but what I *do* know for certain is that my eating disorder nearly destroyed me.

When things first got rough, I ate everything, and I was ashamed. I was heavy, and I felt heavy. I would wear a T-shirt in the wave pool, and while I will say now that it helped with blocking out harmful UV rays, it screamed one thing at the time: fat kid is ashamed of being fat, but still wants to splash around at Dollywood for his family's first and only vacation.

I gained so much weight that gym class became my personal hell. I was reluctant to change in the locker room, and any physical activity was excruciatingly embarrassing. I felt that I was good at nothing, but the absolute worst days were when we had to run. The first time we had to run a mile in sixth grade, the classes I had leading up to my gym period were spent in a full-on panic. It was a timed event, and with the blast of a whistle, I immediately fell to the back of the pack with the rest of the overweight kids. We felt a collective shame as we were lapped by the fast kids with good builds. I developed an immediate and deep self-loathing when, halfway through, I couldn't run any longer. Heaving, I slowed to a walk. I heard the screams of my gym teacher, berating me for being physically unable to go on. The slowest in the class, I finished my mile at eleven minutes and one second, a time that was branded into my mind as embarrassing, pitiful, and disgusting. I hated myself.

In seventh grade, I decided that I was done being fat. I was 130 pounds at the start of the year, heavy for my height. I got a membership to the local YMCA, where I ran and lifted weights before school every morning. My parents supported me, thinking I was just getting in better shape, but what they didn't know was that while I was overexercising, I was also undereating.

Now I was bingeing on exercise and starvation. While I still packed a lunch every day in front of my parents, I'd throw it in the garbage as soon as I got to school. Every day I'd sit at the lunch table with my friends, and in place of a healthy lunch, I'd eat a small pile of pickles from the condiment station in the lunchroom. I was attempting to trick my body into thinking it was getting a meal, for almost zero calories. With my skipped breakfast, before-school workout, pickle lunch, and midday gym class, I was consuming nearly zero calories while burning as many as possible. This is not a good idea.

At dinner, controlling my food intake at home was easy. With so many kids in the family, we ate only one meal a week together—a family movie night, buffet-style. I'd get up and get "seconds," but just rearrange my plate a bit. I was fixated on getting away with my diet, not once acknowledging to myself that it could in some way harm me. Looking back, I see the extreme precautions I took to keep it a secret demonstrate that I knew how wrong it was.

I was constantly exhausted and always dizzy, but in my head I was suffering to get to where I wanted to be in life. If I hated Fat Tyler, then maybe I'd love Skinny Tyler. I had no patience to become the new me in a healthy way, and in a little more than a month I lost thirty pounds and became a skeletal version of myself. Although my ribs protruded and my waist was smaller than ever before, all I could see were problem areas. I'd look in the mirror and cry, disgusted. Yeah, sure, I'd lost some weight, but I could still lose more. And if losing all that weight didn't make me happy yet, maybe if I lost five more pounds? That might work. It was worth a try. Every stomach gurgle felt like a cry of surrender from my body, but I wasn't here to show mercy to something that had caused me years of pain.

Then people started talking. During that month, I changed

my bowl-cut hairstyle and started to gel up my bangs—a popular look for kids my age at the time. I revamped my wardrobe and got rid of my glasses for contacts, thinking people might like me more if I looked less nerdy. I hated who I used to be, and I wanted everything about Fat Tyler to be destroyed. I transformed so much that one day my science teacher did a double take and told me she genuinely thought a new student had transferred into her class. I was ecstatic, at least for the moment, thinking Skinny Tyler was finally here.

When my parents realized I had a problem, it was too late. I had spiraled out of control and was thinner than ever before. My face had sunk in, and none of my clothes fit me. Not knowing what to do or how to help, my parents sent me to therapy, where I sat in silence, refusing to speak. I was in control now, and I wasn't about to let anyone force me to go back to who I used to be. My parents took me to weekly weigh-ins with a doctor, and if that week I hadn't gained weight, I was grounded. Most weeks, I chose being grounded over gaining a pound.

All day long, I thought about food. At the same time, I felt that if anyone saw me eating, I'd be seen as the disgusting Fat Tyler I was terrified to revert back into. Sometimes after a long week of starving myself, I'd sneak into the kitchen in the middle of the night and lose control. With the rest of my family asleep, I'd silently remove the cover from a tray of cake and eat it bite by bite. I'd glide my fork carefully along the side of the cake, attempting to leave absolutely zero proof that I had eaten it. I'd continue this for the entire circumference of the cake, and while it would probably have been easier to just slice myself a piece, people would have noticed. If I was careful enough, if I left no marks, nobody would know I had indulged the night before. My heart pounded with the thought of someone's waking up and finding me. The only thing worse than anyone's realizing the next day some of the cake was gone would've been being caught in the act, so I worked frantically in my surreptitious gluttony. In minutes, I'd devour small bits and pieces of leftovers in the fridge, snacks in the cupboard, and baked goods on the counter. Coming down from my frantic binge blackout, I felt excruciating shame. I had just undone all my hard work and discipline for the week, and I hated myself even more because of it.

The year I developed anorexia was the worst year of my life. I found that it didn't matter if I was Fat Tyler or Skinny Tyler. I still hated myself. While before I couldn't run because I was overweight, now I couldn't run because I got dizzy from exhaustion. I had gone from one extreme to another, neither bringing me any closer to happiness. To make matters worse, I felt that everyone was yelling at me about my weight, telling me how I just needed to eat more, or how I was going to destroy my body, or how I was acting out or causing problems. I felt that nobody understood what I was going through, myself included.

I was in a downward spiral of starvation, weigh-ins, and therapy, practically being force-fed, and hating myself. Near the end, I began to throw bulimia into the mix. I was addicted to control, to the point where I lost any semblance of it.

And then, my choir teacher saved me. Ms. Borton asked me to stay for a moment after class one day, and I instantly knew it was about my weight. Before then, I had generally tried to blend in among the rest of the choir, never trying out for a solo or singing loud enough to stand out. When I went into her office after class, she closed the door behind me.

Ms. Borton was meant to be a teacher. She's who you hope your kids have when they go to school. It was because of her that I fell in love with music, and although I've never been incredibly vocally gifted, she gave me the courage to sing at all the karaoke bars I visit today (sorry, Koreatowns everywhere, blame her).

At the end of class every Friday, Ms. Borton would read us *Chicken Soup for the Soul* chapters, and she taught us the importance of random acts of kindness. We'd take turns giving shout-outs to people in class who had treated us kindly. Her mantra was Singing Produces Awesome Miracles, and she wore SPAM merchandise to constantly remind us of the power of music. She was goofy and hilarious, but intensely serious when she needed to be. She talked to us gently, and when you spoke to her, she heard you, in every sense.

Her office was lined with school pictures of past students, hundreds of kids who had connected with her over the years. She was one of those teachers everyone loved, who made every student feel like the favorite. That day, when I needed it most, I felt like the favorite. She smiled at me with a pained expression that said she already knew the answer to the question she was about to ask.

"Are you okay?"

I immediately started crying. For what felt like the first time in the entire ordeal, someone had approached me with no judgment. Doctors scolded me for mistreating my body, and while I know my parents cared deeply for me, they also made me feel shame for what I was doing, and I felt that they just didn't understand. Sobbing, I didn't know what to say, and she got up, hugged me, and I cried into her shoulder.

I wasn't okay, but Ms. Borton did what she could to help. She got me more involved in choir and musicals, and although I was already friends with my Twister buddy Dolan, one of the best singers in choir and one of the most popular kids in my grade, she made sure we were always together. We became best friends, and I finally felt that someone other than an adult thought I wasn't half-bad.

Ms. Borton was the catalyst for my recovery, but I wouldn't have gotten out of the hole I'd dug for myself without the support of friends and family, as well as a lot of hard work inside my own brain. It all happened slowly but surely, and only because I was ready. I began to eat more regularly, exercise less desperately, and develop a routine that focused on health rather than shape or size. It didn't always work, and some days were better than others. I often hated myself and tried to talk myself back into starving, but those days became fewer and farther between, the longer I worked toward recovery.

Plenty of aha moments happened along the road. One of the most important was the realization that I will always be both Fat Tyler and Skinny Tyler. Both are a part of me and have shaped me into who I am today. My attempt to differentiate between them only negated a fraction of the complete me. Over a few years, I eased back into myself and was able to begin finding peace with my body as just Tyler.

My eating disorder never went away for good. As almost anyone who has ever suffered from an eating disorder can probably tell you, it makes a comeback when you least expect it. It wears on you when you try on clothes. It bobs up when everyone wants to get into the hot tub. It barges into the bedroom during sex. It begs to be let back into your life, and it promises that it's the solution for all of your moments of discomfort. And the hard thing is, in your mind, it seems as if it totally could be.

But an eating disorder isn't about how thin you actually are, it's about how you feel in your own skin. When I was starving myself, no number on my scale was ever going to feel like I was done. I'd pinch undetectable fat on my stomach and punish myself relentlessly. My parents would beg me to eat, and I'd look at them as if they were crazy—could they not see what I saw? That was the problem. Every mirror was a twisted funhouse mirror, reflecting not reality, but distortions from my insecurities.

Over time, your brain gets better at flattening out those warped mirrors, and you begin to see yourself for who you

Tyler Oakley ✓
@tyleroakley

I hate my thighs. Note to self, this is why I dont go jean shopping.

25/10/2008 01:43

Tyler Oakley ✓
@tyleroakley

god I love my thighs, they're so huge that I could crush anyone's head/dreams between them, thank you parents, from your genes to my jeans

10/10/2014 18:41

are—whether that's someone who has a few extra curves on their body or not. Your brain also gets better at caring less about what the mirror actually shows, realizing those few extra pounds aren't a matter of life and death. I still deal with this now a decade later, but I'm getting better at it.

In unpacking my self-loathing attitude toward my weight, I've also learned to unpack how I view body image in culture in general. Being larger is okay. Being smaller is okay. Neither will inherently bring you happiness. Size does not always indicate health. Skinny people are not always happy. Fat people are not always lazy. Men are not exempt from any of this. I learned these things over time, despite the messaging in pop culture, media, and advertisements.

My overwhelmingly kind and extremely talented friend Hannah Hart has a piece of art in her office depicting a young girl walking through a forest, side by side with a wolf. Kind of looks like Little Red Riding Hood and the Big Bad Wolf. When Hannah first showed it to me, she talked about how she loved it so much because it depicted the idea of recognizing your inner demons and, instead of running from them, learning to live with them. I always get asked why the background of my phone is a picture of orange chicken; it's my reminder not to run from my wolf anymore.

anything for a dollar

GROWING UP POOR WAS PRETTY SHITTY AT the time, but now that I've lived through it, I wouldn't change a single thing about it. My parents raised me to understand the value of hard work and saving money, and I like to think that because of that I've gotten to where I am today. I also slept my way to the top, so that helped.

From an early age, I had a weird relationship with money. My family always had financial issues; I grew up eating discount lunches, and back-to-school shopping meant hand-me-downs and off-brands. I didn't mind at first, but I eventually began to notice what my peers had, and I became very aware of where my family ranked on the community-income infographic.

To get what I wanted in life, I was raised to work hard and make it happen—starting at infancy. My sister Codi and I were always trying to come up with ways to capitalize on our community. Our eyes were on the prize: a few bucks, no matter the cost. Which is also the credo of a street hooker.

It started simple: we did a summer lemonade stand in our neighborhood. We served the people of our community an over-sugared, overpriced cup of water with a squeeze of lemon juice, no refunds. If you're thirsty, drink it. If you don't like it, fuck off.

Our efforts, like our avarice, were year-round. Winters in Michigan were no less lucrative. In addition to shoveling the driveways of old ladies, I was interested in darker enterprises. I was not above walking my nimble fingers into the piggy banks of a younger demographic. Our stop being the first on the school-bus route, we were always able to claim the seats nearest to the heaters. This made us the de facto gatekeepers of warmth. If our classmates wanted a blast of heat, they'd have to go through us—and it wasn't cheap. In no time, we had a business running. We charged money for time slots to heat up their cold, damp hats, gloves, and scarves. The colder the weather, the more we charged. Supply and demand, bitch—no quarter asked (except literally), and none given. We slaked our terrible thirst for power with the milk money of our peers.

In the autumn, raking leaves for neighbors was an obvious

opportunity. When spring came, we had to get creative. Codi and I upended our brains searching for something, anything, that would make us a buck. With our combined ages now reaching the double digits, our superior abilities bred superior ambitions. We needed a way to offer a commodity to the people for double its actual value. And then *bam*...it hit us: pizza party!

We pooled our birthday and Christmas money and bought a roll of ticket stubs. Like tiny Napoléons, we would divide and conquer: each taking a set of houses, we'd go door-to-door between the hours of 6:00 and 8:00 p.m. to sell tickets to what would be our neighborhood's first community-fostering event.

I, a chubby nine-year-old with a bowl cut parted down the middle, obviously had zero charm. Luck was in short supply when it came to nervously attempting to sell $10 tickets for $5 worth of Little Caesars Hot-N-Ready pizza. No matter how I spun it, I found the deal impossible to close. I did, however, receive some small pity donations from neighbors willing to support the cause, but unwilling to commit to attendance. Whatever, fuck 'em, more pizza for chubby me.

We ended up selling three tickets (to me, my sister, and her friend down the road) and collecting $20 in donations—a total of $50! Taking out the costs of the pizza, soda, plates, cups, napkins, roll of ticket stubs, streamers, and balloons—and then splitting the cash between the two of us, we barely had a profit...but to us, we were fucking *rich*. These shenanigans continued through the years.

Eventually, I made my way to high school, and the stakes got bigger. I could no longer support my tastes with casual neighborhood events. I had things to pay for, and I needed to get a real job. At exactly fourteen years and eight months, I had reached the minimum age for employment in Michigan, and I was ready to work.

My first job was as an Arby's "drive-thru specialist" (my name tag literally said this). It was not glamorous. But at fourteen, my idea of success was minimum wage and an employee discount on roast beef, so I was in heaven. It was a simpler time.

After Arby's, I made a lateral move in the fast-food industry to McDonald's. There, I was able to work not only drive-thru, but also the front register, the fry station, the grill, and the sandwich line. I mastered the Golden Arches. This feat did not go unnoticed, and I quickly became a trainer. After a time, that particular McDonald's became *the* hot-spot location for my peers to work. Everyone was getting a job there. Among the lineup were my three best friends—Rachel, Dolan, and Eric—all four of us in sand-brown uniforms and black, nonslip shoes. We were basically a gang to be respected and feared, and every day I left work reeking of grease. *Even in high school I was a catch.*

My favorite moment while working at McDonald's (besides when I made out with a bi-curious coworker in the walk-in freezer) happened the summer after I graduated from high school. Mason Brinston was spacey, eccentric, and relatively squirrelly to begin with, so an eight-hour shift in the summer heat didn't necessarily bring out his best. Our store had two drive-thru lanes, and it took four people to run them: two at the first window (one to take orders, one to take money) and two at the second window (one to fill orders, and one to hand them out). One brick goes missing, and the arches crumble. In the middle of the lunchtime rush, Mason was taking orders for both lanes, and I was taking money right next to him.

Some said he may have been on drugs. Others thought he may have had a mental breakdown. But on that day, for reasons still undetermined, Mason cracked.

Traffic was bumper-to-bumper, and we were trying to move the drive-thru line as best as we could. As seasoned pros, both Mason and I knew what we were doing, but when food orders start to get mixed up or cars get out of order, things get messy and tense. Screams from the kitchen, yelling from our manager, and angry customers just might have been the perfect storm. All of a sudden, Mason calmly turned to me, his lips curled into a smile, and took off his headset. Next, Mason climbed out of the drive-thru window. It was only noon, and I was already having my best shift ever.

He quit then and there, not in a fit of frustration or anger, but laughing like a maniac. He removed his regulation clip-on tie while walking between honking cars in the drive-thru line. In the parking lot, he threw his arms up in surrender as if to say, "You win this round, Ronald!" All of us were mystified, but Mason and his empty summer schedule had the last laugh.

My next high school job was working for a coffee shop called Beaners. I hesitate even to write that word now, but that was the name. In my defense, I had no idea the word was a racial slur. In Michigan, we had incredibly few Latinos, and only when the franchise expanded farther south did the management realize that their name was deeply offensive to the fastest-growing population group in the United States. I just thought it was a play on coffee beans.

I was the company's first male barista. After so much time making fast food, I was done with roast beef and moved on to . . . roast beans. In my short time as a barista, I gained about ten pounds from blended hazelnut coffee drinks with way too much whipped cream, and I became obsessed with the drama between my two bosses: a married couple comprised of a husband who was having an affair with a barista, and an angry wife who had no idea. They hated each other, and I lived for it.

It should be noted that I was once the subject of a bidding war between Beaners and McDonald's, and that my ex-manager from McDonald's requested a secret meeting with me in which she offered me whatever Beaners was paying, and then some. You heard right: I was *that* valuable to the mid-Michigan fast-food industry.

Although teens usually complain about having to work, it was the best time of my life. Working through high school gave me the discipline I needed to apply for college—despite knowing it would cost me an arm and a leg—and to then attempt to pay 100 percent of my own way through by working multiple jobs, all while taking classes. Without that foundation, I'd never have had the work ethic to be my own boss today, as a full-time YouTuber. That, and I love free fast food.

After high school, I went off to study at Michigan State University, where I would soon find myself cankle deep in student debt. I worked several jobs throughout my time in school, many at the same time, just to have enough money to pay for my loans, buy books for class, and afford a weekly half gallon of Popov.

If I had to pick one job during my time at university that was my shining moment, it would indisputably be telemarketing. Nightly, I'd go into a fluorescent-lit call center, surrounded by two hundred other starving college students. For a few hours, I would call alumni, begging for donations to the colleges at which they had studied. In hindsight, who knows why they needed us to beg alumni, most of whom were still paying off their debt? I didn't care—as long as my own paycheck cleared.

It took me no time to realize that my God-given talent was convincing people to give me their money. In minutes, I could sweet-talk jaded alumni, whose microwave dinners I had interrupted with my call, into signing up to be monthly donors. I could woo them into joining our Spartan level of philanthropists, giving a $100 onetime donation, or even something as binding as an ongoing monthly pledge of $10. It didn't matter how much debt they were in, if they didn't get me off the phone in the first minute, I had them and their cash in my pocket.

My specialty was elderly women—whether they realized I was gay, I don't know, but I could sing them the song their busy grandchildren never took time to sing. I'd call, ask them about their days, their weeks, their lives. I'd want to know about their stories, their husbands, their grandchildren, their dreams and aspirations, what made them laugh, their favorite soap operas, how many times they'd voted for David Archuleta on *American Idol* last week, *anything* to keep them talking. As long as I had them on the phone for a while, they'd open up their purses and find their checkbooks.

Now, before you think I was taking advantage of these poor old ladies, realize this: *they* were the ones using *me*. I had calls to make and goals to reach, and they, with their slow drawls and faltering memories, were taking up *my time*! I couldn't help it that I had a mandate that came along with each geriatric gossip session. As soon as I realized I could see who I was next randomly assigned to call, I started cheating the system. If my next call wasn't to someone born before 1950, I would immediately push "no answer" and move on to the next call in the system. I was "only here for grandmas."

Although I'm not typically competitive, my position as the granny whisperer in the telemarketing room boosted me to top caller, number one out of about two hundred people, for two weeks in a row. To this day, I have an internal debate over whether that should be my Twitter bio.

During my sophomore year of university, my YouTube presence began to slowly grow, and with that, a man named Garth from the campus career-services center found my videos. His daughter, a classmate of mine from high school, was watching them in her kitchen. He looked over her shoulder, asked who I was, and found out that I was a student at the university that he worked at. He reached out, asked me to come in for a meeting, and immediately offered me a position running their digital presence and student outreach on social media. The job was basically to make videos about how to get a job, how to write a résumé, interview tips, and other career advice. I didn't have any experience, but they gave me a free computer and paid me more than the telemarketing job, so I said yes.

The gig gave my online presence a bit of a local push, as my career videos were played to lecture halls and for incoming freshmen at orientation. Posters with my face were plastered all over campus, reaffirming all of my insecurities every time I turned a corner. For a brief stint, a mobile-billboard truck was even driving around campus with my face on it. Sorry, no autographs.

Once, times got really tough, and I started selling plasma for cash. Basically, they draw your blood, take the plasma out of it, then put what's left back in you . . . *all for like twenty bucks!* Listen, I was poor in college. I remember one time, I went out to the bar one night, got drunk, and ended up going home with a guy. For the walk of shame the next morning, I had to run *two miles* in flip-flops to make it back to the car pool to go donate plasma. University was an interesting time.

As the years went on, I picked up a bunch of jobs. I was a busy boy. As a teacher's assistant for public speaking, I had three classes of freshmen students presenting speeches that I would grade them on. During summers, I was a sports-camp counselor. I also spent three of my school years as an RA, a resident mentor in the dorms. Even with all these jobs, I still graduated asshole-deep in debt. The American higher education system is *fucked*. Nearing graduation with no job prospects, which wasn't the best position to be in, I started to panic . . . but more on how I dug myself out of that hole later.

disney princes

DON'T ACT LIKE YOU DIDN'T HAVE A CRUSH ON an animated character when you were growing up. I did. I had plenty! Heck, in 1997, T.J. Detweiler from *Recess* was my celebrity crush. But when it came to cartoon men, I was all about the Disney princes. Please enjoy my definitive ranking.

12. TIE FOR LAST PLACE: PRINCE PHILLIP / PRINCE FLORIAN (*Sleeping Beauty / Snow White*)—On one hand, we've got Phillip from *Sleeping Beauty*, who slew a dragon for his lady, and on the other hand, Florian from *Snow White*, who clearly is comfortable with lots of short men living intimately together (my dream) . . . but I'm not into boys who give nonconsensual kisses. Sure, he had good intentions, but, like, don't kiss me in my sleep. It's a simple ground rule. You don't know if those ladies wanted that. Maybe they were having a good dream. Maybe they were dreaming about Darren Criss. You don't know what you just interrupted. Rude.

11. TRAMP (*Lady and the Tramp*)—This dog may not be a Disney prince, but any guy who wants to go splitsies on spaghetti and meatballs? Woof.

10. PRINCE CHARMING (*Cinderella*)—This guy is way too materialistic, with absolutely no personality. In the movie, he's the definition of blah and has a shoe fetish. Don't get me wrong, I enjoy a solid pair of TOMS, but glass slippers? Not my style. What if you have a blister, corns, or a hammertoe? You can see that right through those slippers. NAGL (not a good look). Also, Cinderella never even said she wanted a husband. All she asked for was a night out of the house to go dancing. She didn't ask for your golden handcuffs, self-proclaimed Prince Charming.

9. JOHN SMITH (*Pocahontas*)—*He has a mullet.* I mean, at least he can kind of rock it, but I'm pretty sure his hairstyle was what *Savages* was written about—barely even human, rotten at the core.

8. BEAST (*Beauty and the Beast*)—Don't get me wrong, I like a hairy chest . . . but everyone has their limits.

7. FLYNN RIDER (*Tangled*)—I like a man who is unapologetically himself. If you gotta go around with a fake name . . . then you need to get on my level. Call me when you're ready, Eugene Fitzherbert.

6. PINOCCHIO (*Pinocchio*)—I like his no-strings-attached attitude, but I'm not looking for a real boy—I'm looking for a real *man*.

5. ERIC (*The Little Mermaid*)—You may be wondering why one of the *hottest* Disney princes of all time is ranked so low. . . . Well, let's just say he's done a bad thing . . . and not in a good way. Sure, he's got the body and the eyes (yes, I'm talking this way about a cartoon), but he *killed* the *best* Disney villain of all time, the drag queen that is Ursula. Unforgivable. RIP.

4. LI SHANG (*Mulan*)—Though it's never clearly stated in the film, Li Shang might be a bit bi-curious, given that he seemed into Mulan when he knew her as Ping. . . . He might be the only Disney prince I actually have a chance with—and his body ain't half-bad. Plus a bit of discipline and ambition? He could make a man out of me.

3. NAVEEN (*The Princess and the Frog*)—Okay, sometimes Prince Naveen comes across a bit smarmy, but he's also tall, dark and handsome—*plus*, royalty (!!!). And I've got to agree with Tiana, he's lacking in work ethic, but I think with a little growing up . . . I'd hop on that.

2. KRISTOFF (*Frozen*)—I typically go for a guy my size, but there's something lovable about a big, burly man. Honestly, I'm just looking for a big spoon on a cold winter's night—and I think I've got what it takes to prove to Kristoff that people are, in fact, better than reindeer.

1. ALADDIN (*Aladdin*)—Yaas. Sure he's got some problems with the law—but who doesn't love a bad boy? Any guy who is willing to go to *jail* for some carbs? Ooo, I think he's rather tasty, and he ain't ever had a (boy)friend like me.

brace yourself

W HEN MY PARENTS FORCED ME TO GET
braces in middle school, I was furious . . . until I
met the man who was going to be tightening them
every four to six weeks. My parents were cheap, so they drove
me an hour away to the campus of the University of Michigan. Dental students used poor kids like me as their practice
dummies, and when I met mine, I was ready to surrender all
control. My student was tall, handsome, charming, and had
muscles bulging under his scrubs. He had to be more than a
decade older than me, but that didn't stop me from thirsting.
I'd lie back, mouth stretched open, our faces just inches apart.
I'd be positioned upside down, as in that kiss in the *Spider-Man*
movie, looking deep into his beautiful brown eyes, hoping he
would feel the connection.

One day during a particularly intimate tightening, my orthodontist was busy tinkering on the brackets attached to each
tooth while I daydreamed about our life together. In our future,
he'd work all day making children cry for not wearing their re-

tainers, but as soon as he walked through our front door, all his worries would dissipate. We'd adopt children together, and our entire family would have perfect teeth, under his careful supervision.

"Spit," he'd say every few minutes, each time jolting me from my daydream. Our conversations were always like this—short, sweet, and usually telling me to spit. Whatever, I felt the connection.

On that day, as I looked up into his eyes, something made me lose all control. I thought, *You know what? I should probably make a move before our final appointment.* So, I did what any twelve-year-old flirting with a man twice his age might do—I licked his fingers.

In a flash, he withdrew them from my mouth, and his eyes fixed on mine. ". . . Do you . . . need to spit?"

"No."

Maybe a second of awkward silence passed, maybe it was three, but it felt like an eternity. I had blown my chances, and I was mortified. We never did fall in love, and I felt weird each time I returned for future tightenings. When I got my braces off, my hot orthodontist student and I parted ways for good. Eventually, I lost my retainer and my teeth shifted back to their original crooked state. Maybe I misplaced it by accident, or maybe subconsciously I just wanted to get back into his reclined dental chair.

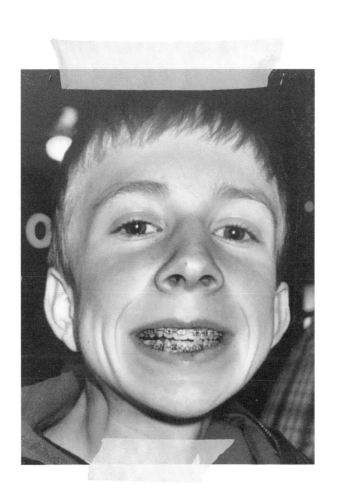

the t-mobile incident

MY MOM HAS NEVER BOUGHT INTO THE Holly-wood glamour aspect of my YouTube life. Sure, she brags about my accomplishments to all of her Face-book friends, but no matter how many celebrity interviews I conduct, red-carpet events I work, or big, important meetings I have, I'm still her Michigan boy just doing his job. Although she has always been my biggest fan, she and the rest of my family don't let a single aspect of my career go to my head, and they haven't done so since my first humble beginnings.

I refer to a time before I ever had a smartphone, a laptop, or even a video camera. I was baffled by the most basic editing software, and because this was before Tumblr existed, I didn't have so much as an outlet to complain about it.

My most advanced piece of technology back then was my flip phone. Flip phones were standard for all of my peers when we were in high school, and I got my first just in time for them to become outdated, putting me years behind when I entered college. The most popular version was called a Razr, and on top of being late to the flip-phone game, I was also too poor to afford anything but the knockoff. My model was thick, clunky, and went by a sleek name that rolled right off the tongue: the W490.

This was before cell phone cases even existed, so the W490 came in a vast multitude of colors, including bubble-gum pink, kiwi green, and a subtle plum. Because these phones had a quirky level of reliability unlike any other phone on the market, they came in bulk packs. As soon as one inevitably glitched or stopped working altogether, you could just switch your battery and SIM card into another phone. I was truly living the life of high-tech luxury.

It should also be noted that before phones had every letter displayed on their touch screens, you had to press the number-pad buttons. To text, you had to use a system called T9 texting—with the letters being evenly divided among all the numbers. I would explain the process in more depth, but those were dark times, and I'd rather not go down that rabbit hole, even mentally.

I was used to my phone's breaking down or having minimal battery life, but for some reason, one of my models had issues with its keypad whenever I would attempt to use T9 texting. Frustrated with the mediocre quality of a mediocre phone for which I paid minimal money, I decided enough was enough. I'd confront the local, part-time employees of T-Mobile and demand answers as soon as possible—or at least whenever my mom could give me a ride to the store, since I didn't have a car.

My mom and I pulled up to the bleak strip mall, and I stormed into T-Mobile with the fury of a crazy cat lady con-

vinced that not only does the cat food in *this* can taste off, but also that the clerk in the store she bought it from had everything to do with the problem.

"Hi, my phone seems to be having some issues?"

"Can you describe the problem?"

"Well, anytime I text, it freezes and then shuts down?"

"Have you tried restarting it?"

"Obviously . . ."

This volley of questions went on back and forth until one of us caved and finally offered a declarative statement.

"Well," he said, "the W490 model isn't really made for texting."

I stared at this man. In any other circumstance, I probably wouldn't have hated him with a smoldering passion. We might have been cordial acquaintances, perhaps even friends—but this was not to be.

Fuming, I slowly asked, "Then why . . . does the phone . . . offer *texting* as a feature?"

"Ahhh, it's just not recommended with this model. Honestly, we're just a retailer, and since this model is so old that we don't carry it anymore, I can't really speak to its functionality."

"Right, well, I need to be able to text to be able to do *my job*. . . . I need to tweet—and to tweet, I need to be able to *text*." Back then, there was no Twitter app, only the option to text your tweets to the phone number 40404. Times were tough.

"Have you thought about getting a Razr?"

I winced. Oh, had that not occurred to me? Every. Single. Day? Had I not dreamed, plotted, fantasized, coveted, schemed, lost hope, found it again, and started the whole cycle anew? Thanks for asking. Yes, I've thought about getting a Razr. But I'm *poor*, and not only that, but I've invested in *a six-pack* of these W490 pieces of *shit*.

Maybe it was a bad day. Maybe I woke up on the wrong side of the bed. Maybe I had a time-sensitive, career-defining tweet in my head that I couldn't text to Twitter because my phone kept freezing up. Maybe I'm just an asshole, and this day doubly so. But thanks to my better judgment, I was able to recognize that today was not the day to escalate an argument in my local T-Mobile retail store. I swiveled my glare from the T-Mobile employee toward my mom, who was standing mutely on the sidelines, eyebrows raised.

"Come on, Mom, this guy does *not* know what he's talking about."

I stomped my way back through the T-Mobile store, toward the exit, with my mom in tow a few paces behind me. Although I felt shame for throwing a tantrum in public, I was about to leave the situation, and I could soon act as if none of it had ever happened.

I reached for the door, feeling my agitation beginning to fade and my composure returning. That's when I heard my mom's voice behind me, mocking my behavior: "Do you have *any* idea who he is? My son is a *YouTube celebrity*, and you will be *hearing about this*."

I cringed. As much as you might have just cringed reading that, I cringed a thousand times more. In that moment, I realized I was the worst of the world's entitled brats. I'd bought the shittier version of the phone I actually wanted, and I'd received the exact product and service I'd paid for. My mom didn't raise me to abuse strangers just because I don't get my way. I went from feeling like an empowered hot-shit consumer advocate to a self-important schmuck in one second flat. Just when I thought it couldn't get worse, I attempted to push open T-Mobile's door and exit. It wasn't budging. Was it locked? What the *fuck*? Gently, my mom demonstrated how to pull the door open, rather than pushing it.

We made our way through the parking lot in silence. When we got back into her car, she looked over at me before turning the key in the ignition. "You done throwing a fit?"

"Yeah," I groaned.

I learned a few valuable lessons that day. First, don't be a dick. Second, if you're frustrated with a situation you put yourself in, stop blaming others. Finally, a good mom is supportive of you, but the best moms are supportive of your *growth*. Even when it doesn't seem like they're on your side, great mothers are on the side of your becoming a better person, and you'll be so much better off in the long run. So pull out your flip phone and text to 40404 a quick thank-you to your mom. She has your best interests at heart, even if you *are* sometimes a dick.

all the world's a stage

"All the world's a stage." —William Shakespeare
—Tyler Oakley, 2007

AT THE AGE OF FIVE, I HIT THE STAGE FOR THE first time. It was a kindergarten production of *Teddy Bears' Picnic*, and mine was not a speaking part. I sang in the chorus, seething over the attention (and costumes!) the leads got. On the bright side, I was completely relieved that I didn't have to memorize any lines. This theme dominated my entire dramatic career: I could never remember lines.

I was so bad at memorizing lines that nonspeaking roles became my calling. During the summer months of elementary school, I hung out at home with all of my siblings, suffering through the heat while trying to find something to do. This was during the golden era of a TV show on Nickelodeon called *All That*. It was basically *Saturday Night Live*, but made by and for kids.

My siblings and I loved *All That* so much that we would reenact our favorite skits and perform them for our parents. While my older brothers and sisters had no problem memorizing scripts, I was hopeless. Thankfully, from seasons one to six and again for a brief stint in season ten, one of the recurring characters on *All That* was a Big Ear of Corn—just a human-size vegetable prop. As I stood entirely still in a bright yellow turtleneck and green overalls, becoming the most convincing ear of corn my parents' basement had ever seen, I beamed with pride. Obviously, my dedication to the craft was yielding dividends.

After the overwhelming success of my first stage performance in Teddy Bears' Picnic, I decided to take a brief hiatus from professional productions. This was intended, obviously, to build suspense for an impending comeback and to give an aura of mystery to my brand. My efforts were abetted by my attending a poor school that didn't have a fine arts program or budgets for plays or musicals. Not until fifth grade, when I went on to middle school, did my school's budget (and the public's insatiable need) dictate my return to the stage.

When my middle school announced that *Jack and the Beanstalk* would be its next production, I saw that this was my chance to play the lead. I was ten years old and had a heart brimming with big dreams. Back then, I believed that if I wanted something badly enough, it would come to be. It was basically The Secret, and no less effective (which is to say, not at all).

There's a quote about shooting for the moon, and how even if you miss, you'll land among the stars. Whoever said that doesn't understand the size of outer space. Nonetheless, I shot for the moon during my audition for *Jack and the Beanstalk*, and I did indeed land among the stars. I didn't get the title role, but my extensive acting experience as the Big Ear of Corn had prepared me perfectly for my next role as an inanimate object: one of the forty statues in the Giant's castle.

My performance as a statue was *crucial* to the success of the production. Without me, I'm not sure any of the other actors could have properly *felt* the tone of the show. In my gray-on-gray sweatpants and sweater, I stood absolutely still. So still that a chill spread over the audience. As a single statue among forty, I changed the acting game. They say there are no small parts, only small actors. At four feet one inch, I was both.

That year, I had a lot of far-fetched dreams that I just assumed would happen. I remember one day in particular, I was completely positive that I was going to end the day as a millionaire. While I typically alternated between homemade cold lunches and reduced-price hot lunches, for the first time ever my parents splurged and bought me a real, authentic, brand-name Lunchables. I felt disgustingly, filthy rich.

Having never had a Lunchables before, I sat in the back-seat on my way to school studying the rules and regulations of the contest on that particular box. Positive that my Lunchables contained the golden ticket, my stepdad and I agreed that upon my discovering my win, I was to inconspicuously rise from my seat at the lunch table, walk calmly to the office, cardboard box in hand, and feign sickness. Only in the privacy of my dad's car was I to celebrate my newly won riches. I regret to inform you that I didn't win that contest. But I did get to eat three mini-pizzas and a Capri Sun that day. Shoot for the moon, land among the stars.

After discovering the comfort of acting in sweatpants, I was bitten by the performance bug. I relocated my talents from the lost age of giant beanstalks to the 1920s, for a production called *Flapper*. It had a lot of rhyming of the words *flapper* and *dapper*, and even more jazz squares. Who doesn't love a period piece? I auditioned immediately and got the role of a lifetime: Newsboy #1.

Back when I was one of forty statues, I could easily blend in and go unnoticed. As one of four newsboys, well, I can only describe it like Britney Spears did in her hit single "Circus": all eyes on me / in the center of the ring / just like a circus.

Unfortunately, the primary reason all eyes were on me was that the roles of the newsboys were created specifically to give the crew time to change the stage sets.

My lines were interstitial to actual scenes relevant to the musical. To give historical context to the plot, I recited 1920s headlines, newspaper in hand. Stop the presses! Given that this was my first role with lines, I was petrified on opening night. I was so nervous that, as I paced backstage before the show, my mind went completely blank. In a frenzy, I scrambled to find a pen, and I scribbled each and every line onto the palms of my hands.

When the first set change came, it was my moment to shine. I exploded onto the side of the auditorium, clutching my newspaper, and a single spotlight knifed through the darkness and fixed upon me. It was all very "Seasons of Love" from *Rent*. Spread throughout the rest of the auditorium, I saw my fellow newsboys step into spotlights of their own. We were ready to take turns reciting our headlines, starting first, logically, with Newsboy #1.

My voice shook as I yelled out the first half of my line, an easily remembered *"Extra! Extra! Read all about it!"* As soon as I looked down into the palm of my hand for the second half, my heart dropped. My nervous sweat had smudged my headline, and I stood there, paralyzed. I knew one of us had to say *something* about the stock market crashing, so I just screamed, *"The stock market crashed!"*

Across the auditorium, Newsboy #3's face went pale. He looked at me, wide-eyed and mouth agape. Uh-oh. I took his line. Thankfully, Newsboy #3 was lightning on his feet, and he was able to extemporize another headline. I wonder what ever happened to Newsboy #3. Did my blunder spark his interest in improv? Maybe someday he'll be cast on *SNL*, and in press releases he'll cite my abundant palm sweat as the catalyst of his career? You're *welcome*, Newsboy #3.

From this role, I learned a lesson about the importance of permanent markers, as well as to never combine a bowl haircut with a newsboy cap. I was evolving in my craft.

That year, I joined my fellow seventh graders for a week-long trip to camp. We bundled up in snowsuits and were baby-sat by high schoolers who volunteered to be camp counselors. My counselor, Stephen Carrasco, was flamboyant, theatrical, and everything that I—short, pudgy, closeted seventh grader Tyler Oakley—wished I could be. He was in the Someko Singers (my school district's AP choir, named by the reverse spelling of our hometown) and got plenty of leading roles in the musicals at the high school. Seeing him be unapologetically himself, un-ashamed and openly gay, all while being successful and popu-lar, gave me hope. Maybe someday I too could tell my friends and family the truth about who I was and it would be far from the end of the world. Last I heard, he was in *Kinky Boots* on Broadway. Slay me.

After *Flapper*, my second low-budget middle-school pro-duction was *Wagon Wheels West*, a musical spoof of the west-ern genre. I played Josiah Aimless, a farmer from New England, traveling across the land hoping to strike gold in California. Given that this was a much bigger role than anything I'd previ-ously done, I decided that a named character deserved a back-story. I began to fantasize about Josiah Aimless's complicated past. In the script, he was married with kids, but my Josiah Aimless was bi-curious for sure, and his fears included mea-sles, snakebites, dysentery, typhoid, cholera, and exhaustion, or basically any way you can die in the game *The Oregon Trail*.

Trying to remember the details of a bad, forgettable musi-cal for the sake of this book is like torture. But jogging my mem-ory by watching clips of middle-school productions of *Wagon Wheels West* on the Internet? Delightful.

I don't remember much about the musical itself, but I remember like yesterday that I was in love with the guy who played the lead: Dan Byrne. He got all the solos in choir and the lead in the play, and I got nothing because my voice wasn't done cracking and I couldn't remember lines. Obviously, we were archrivals. He was also on the soccer team, and since we had gym class together, I was made privy to how he'd gone through puberty much sooner (and better) than I did. He eventually moved away and attended a private boarding school for high school, and years later we reunited randomly and had a heart-to-heart in the backseat of his car. We discovered that we had hated each other because secretly we were jealous of each other—me of his talents, and him of my ability to get along with the rest of the school. Unfortunately, that heart-to-heart didn't end with a make-out sesh, which sucks.

Tyler Oakley @tyleroakley

a very very strange night with my arch nemesis from middle school... some people never change... but when they do, it's a nice surprise

RETWEETS 4   FAVORITES 7

1:58 AM - 2 May 2008

Moving on to high school was like advancing into the big leagues. By that, I mean the Drama Club had a budget, and we could do shows that people had actually heard of. I was eager to stretch beyond being a bisexual, dysentery-fearing settler or numbered newsboy.

Okemos High School's art wing was as far as possible from any academic classroom. Over my four years of high school, it became the perfect escape from full days of tedious academia. The greenroom was the coziest room in the whole school. There, on the worn couch in the back of the room, many drama kids had been dared into their first awkward kisses. Posters from every past production hung like pennants around the circumference of the room, reminding the upperclassmen of their glory days. I was eager to distinguish my own era by delivering one incredible portrayal after another of various inanimate objects.

I remember walking into the greenroom for my first time. I was too nervous to talk to any of the many upperclassmen, but I attempted to mingle. Mostly, I was just trying to take it all in. The upperclassmen were ducking in and out of the department's extraordinary costume closet, emerging in wigs and corsets or sporting swords and beards. We could be whoever we wanted, both on and off the stage. Sure, we had tons of fun performing musicals and plays for audiences, but in the time spent *not* performing I figured out who I was. I got to wear a lot of makeup, there were plenty of sexually ambiguous guys, and we had unmonitored computers lining one of the walls. Heaven.

Throughout my years in the Okemos drama program, I began to get roles with lines that were nontrivial to the plot of the show. I was Eugene in *Grease*, excelling at portraying a socially awkward dweeb, mainly because I was already those things. I went back to my roots as an inanimate object in *Beauty and the Beast*, where I played Cogsworth, the tightly wound and persnickety clock. I was painfully in love with my candelabra counterpart, Lumière, and would stew in fury while watching him make out backstage with Babette, the feather duster. Tyler Oakley: third-wheeling since 1989.

I was Nicolas in *The Legend of Sleepy Hollow* and Fenton in *The Merry Wives of Windsor*, both of which I have zero recollection of now, ten years later. I was the Vizier in *Arabian Nights*. I got to put on a wig and a dress and be as creepy as humanly possible as the Pardoner in *The Canterbury Tales*, which was borderline typecasting.

My all-time favorite show had to be *The Importance of Being Earnest*. I was cast as Algernon, who was wittiness and aestheticism personified—everything I dreamed of becoming. It was the first time my two best friends (who later went on to study musical theater in college) couldn't audition for a show. While I typically got bronze, with them out of the picture I was upgraded to gold. I fell in love with the show, probably because I had the best lines. While memorizing lines had always been impossible for me before, this time it was like learning a 1890s drag queen's witty catchphrases, and I couldn't get enough. I also got to wear this incredible maroon, three-piece suit that I bought at the local Goodwill for $3.99. I still have it; it's in my parents' garage. Maybe I'll wear it to a book signing in your town.

Another favorite production was *Into the Woods*, in which I was the Narrator. Considering I had my own library nook on the side of the stage and even got to hold a book as if I were reading the story to the audience, I decided to not learn one damn line. Instead, I wrote out every single one in my narrator's book. As was tradition on opening night of Okemos High School productions, the crew fucked with the actors by taping porn to the props. No baby doll's face or hand mirror was safe. On this opening night, I was horrified to find that the crew had covered the lines in my book with anime tentacle porn. Luckily, my lines were still there, hidden underneath each mortifying image, but I still was thrown for a loop.

My final performance at Okemos High School was in the role of Nicely-Nicely Johnson in *Guys and Dolls*. I sang a rousing rendition of "Sit Down, You're Rockin' the Boat." To this day, I cringe remembering it. Before opening weekend, we would always do condensed versions of the shows as previews for the entire student body, and for *Guys and Dolls*, the director chose the scene of my solo. Terrified that if I went all out for the school preview, I'd lose my voice before opening night, I decided to whisper-sing my high notes during the school preview. While I thought I was nailing it, apparently I just sounded like the isolated vocals of 2014 Mariah Carey attempting to sing "All I Want for Christmas Is You." How does my drama career end? Not with a bang, but a whisper.

While many of my castmates planned to study acting or musical theater professionally after high school, I decided that I'd give just one last performance before retiring from the stage. At my school's graduation ceremony, I was chosen to speak. Among a litany of other sophomoric clichés, I spoke about how "all the world's a stage." I had no clue how prophetic my speech was to become for my own life.

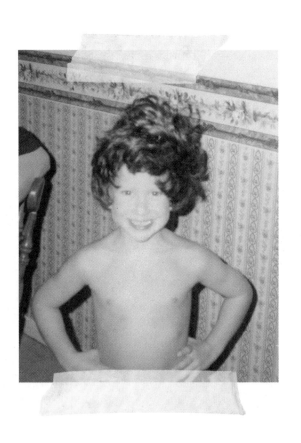

the gay chapter

OMING OUT IS A PROCESS, AND NO LGBTQ+ person is ever done doing it. Although it gets easier to do every time, most of the world is pretty heteronormative and assumes that people are straight by default. Well, newsflash world! I'm (*spoiler!*) gay.

My mom and stepdad always knew. Instead of using words such as *girlfriend* or *wife*, they'd use *significant other* or *partner* to casually let me know that it was okay if I ended up someday riding dick. Not until I was eleven did we ever acknowledge it out loud. That day, my mom and I were in line at the bank. She looked at me and asked if I was gay; I said yes, grabbed a handful of free suckers at the counter, and that was it.

Coming out to my friends was a different story. Going into high school, I knew I was gay, but I had never told anyone outside the family. I kept it to myself for years despite how supportive my surroundings were. My school had a gay-straight alliance club, many out and proud teachers, and plenty of openly gay students, but I just wasn't ready.

When I did come out to my school, it wasn't by choice, and I was far from prepared.

I was nearing the end of a high school production of *Grease*, and the months of long nights of rehearsals meant plenty of free time spent with Eric Maier, a new friend of mine, who was smart, funny, sang well, and was on the soccer team—and I was infatuated. He said he was straight, but sexual speculation was a popular pastime at Okemos High, and I hoped it wasn't true.

Over my freshman year, I began to tell a few friends one by one, but the person I most wanted to tell was Eric. One friend I told was Suzi, who took the news a little too well. She was giddy at the thought of playing matchmaker between Eric and me, but I forbade her to say anything. I wasn't ready! And he could be straight! And she needed to mind her damn business! She assured me that I had nothing to worry about, which I was dumb enough to believe.

The next day was the school preview of our production of *Grease*. It was the Thursday before opening weekend, and we had a midday assembly to do a highlights version of the production, which we hoped would entice the student body to buy tickets. I was in the greenroom caking on some last-minute stage makeup when Suzi rounded the corner, beaming. I scrutinized her suspiciously before returning to my mirror. I opened my eyes as wide as possible and began applying eyeliner. Suzi sat behind me and was outwardly giddy.

"Five minutes until places!" our director called from the other room.

"What mischief are you up to?" I whispered.

"He knows!" she squealed.

I stopped applying my eyeliner and looked at her hard in the reflection of the mirror. "What?" I snapped.

"Eric knows!" Suzi grinned.

"You are unbelievable," I fumed, shaking my head, putting my makeup back into my Ziploc bag. In less than twenty-four hours, Suzi had betrayed my trust and told the one secret I wasn't ready to share to the one person I feared telling most.

"Wait, are you mad at me . . . ?" she began, as I rushed out of the makeup room.

Around the corner and back into the greenroom, I was surrounded by the entire cast of the musical, and a moment away from bursting into tears. As I began to make my way to the door, Eric turned the corner. We made eye contact and my stomach dropped. I brushed past him and opened the auditorium's backstage door.

"Wait, Tyler . . . ," he called, just as the door closed behind me. I was now backstage, in pitch-black darkness, tears streaming down my face. I made my way to center stage and listened to the people chattering on the other side of the curtain, trying to pick up something, anything, that any of them might be saying. Were they talking about it yet? Had their friends texted them the news?

Keep it together, Tyler. Get through this, and you can cry when you get home, I thought, as I wiped my tears from my cheeks. I focused on my breathing until, finally, the curtain began to rise. With all eyes on me, I grinned through my pain and began the musical with the opening monologue.

As soon as the preview was done, I skipped the final bows and ran from backstage through the auditorium door. I slipped into the greenroom and stuffed my clothes into my backpack. Feeling as if I were suffocating, I had to get out of there before the rest of the cast returned. I burst through the school doors and broke down into tears as I crossed the parking lot to my friend's car. She would be giving me a ride home that day, and I sank down against the door of her car, face in my hands, sobbing. As I heard the final bell of the day ring, I wiped my tears as people began to pile out of the school toward the parking lot. When I heard the doors of the car unlock, I stood up and saw my friends approaching. I faked a smile as they congratulated me on the per-formance, and we drove toward our neighborhood.

As soon as I stepped into my house, I let the devastation of the day sweep over me. Eric knew my secret, and he was never going to speak to me again, I was sure of it. I was a disgusting faggot who had been lying to his friends, and soon the entire school was going to know. I lay on the bottom bunk of my bed with my phone in my hand, trying to work up the courage to call Eric. After about an hour of crying and weighing my op-tions, I opened my flip phone and dialed his number. My hands shook as the phone rang.

"Hey . . ."

"Hey . . . ," I started, voice shaking.

"Is everything okay?"

"Suzi told me she told you," I said quickly.

Eric said nothing.

"And I'd rather you hear it from me. . . . I'm gay." Even though I knew he already knew, saying it myself felt final and gave me a sense of relief. No matter what he was going to say next, it was done, and the burden was off my shoulders.

"I know . . . ," Eric began, and the two of us said nothing for what felt like hours, but was probably just seconds. "And, ummm, I think you should know . . . I'm straight. But, like, nothing changes between us. You're still my best friend."

It wasn't the answer I was hoping for, but it was for sure the answer I needed. I thanked him and told him I should probably get back to my homework, and I hung up.

The next morning, I walked into my school, terrified of what might happen. As I walked down the hall, I saw Eric turn the corner and begin walking in my direction. My heart ached and raced and felt like it could burst as we approached each other. As soon as he saw me, a huge grin covered his face, and all doubts left my mind as he opened his arms and hugged me. It was tight and warm and lasted long enough for me to get the message: we're good.

From that point on, coming out was simple. My favorite way to come out was to join a discussion of common lust for hot guys in our classes. Nothing takes a friendship to the next level like a shared thirst. As I told more people at my school, it got easier and easier, until finally I just changed my MySpace and Facebook profiles to say I was interested in men. Just like that, the deed was done. The last thing I had left was to come out to my dad.

My dad is an interesting case. Growing up, I hated him. He was probably the most stubborn person I'd ever met, besides myself, and we fought constantly. He was closed-minded and made it known to me that he wouldn't accept homosexuality in his house.

Catholicism was a huge part of this attitude, and my dad and stepmom worked endlessly to make sure God was always on my mind, instead of dick. Every Tuesday in elementary school, I'd attend Confraternity of Christian Doctrine class, or CCD for short. We learned the Ten Commandments, how to confess our sins, and all the major prayers—but I never bought any of it. When we went through the Lent curriculum, I couldn't believe how many liars were in my class. One kid even had the audacity to claim that he had given up throwing rocks into the river for Lent. I rolled my eyes in between bites of my pączki and sneered, "You have to actually give up something *enjoyable*, idiot," which earned me ten Hail Marys.

The only reason I put up with CCD was so that I could see my crush every Tuesday, a boy whose name I no longer recall, but whose bangs had me mesmerized.

When my dad and stepmom switched from Catholic to New Age Hip Christian, their crusade continued. As part of their attempt to assimilate me into heterosexual teenage-boy culture, they got me a subscription to *Breakaway*—a magazine for teen guys published by the antigay group Focus on the Family. It featured Christian guys talking about their intimate relationships with God and had in-depth articles about how to deal with the temptations of sin. I eagerly anticipated every edition, but only for the fitness section: hot Christian guys showing workout techniques. I definitely sinned every month to that page. Ten more Hail Marys!

By the time I got to high school, I no longer gave a fuck. One day, my dad called and told me he was in town and wanted to grab dinner, and I remember feeling that something was weird. I hadn't seen him for a month or so, and when I walked into Quiznos, he looked noticeably different. It was over a decade ago, but I still remember so clearly the moment he looked up at me as I walked in, seeing his gaunt face and a sad, tired ex-pression. He dove right into the conversation.

He told me someone from his church had found my My-Space page, and how it said I was interested in men. He asked if it was true, I told him yes, and my mind began racing. I was so overwhelmed that I only remember snippets of what he said to me, things suggesting that this was my mom and stepdad's fault, how I was doing this for attention, how this was just a phase, how it was a sin, how he was concerned because I was living a dangerous lifestyle, how it was a choice.

What stuck with me most was his saying he had enough money to fix it. Did he think somehow sending me to therapy could perhaps make me straight? I will never forget his saying that—because it wasn't just the words that were ridiculous, but the tone of it all. It sounded so full of genuine care, said not with anger or disgust, but with love—and this is why homophobia is a terrible evil: it disguises itself as concern while it is inherently hate. I was lucky enough to know this, but so many queer and questioning youth aren't, and almost all homophobic people will outright deny it. No person, no matter how important society deems their relationship to you, has the right to denounce you for who you are.

After that, we never discussed my being gay again, and our relationship was even more nonexistent than before. I saw him at major family events and holidays, but for the most part, we did our own thing. My being gay didn't come up again until several years later while I was in college. I was a couple years into making YouTube videos, and living with a boyfriend at the time, and we were figuring out our holiday plans. As both of us had parents who were divorced and remarried, he and I had four Christmases to attend, and trying to coordinate them all was almost impossible.

When I texted my dad to see when his family was celebrating, I casually mentioned that both my boyfriend and I would be coming. In an instant, the mood switched, and my dad went off. He sent a volley of texts about how I was not allowed to bring that lifestyle to his house, how my YouTube channel was disgracing the family name, and how I'd never get a job. I told him to never text me again unless he was ready to not only accept me for who I was, but proudly embrace everything about me.

We didn't speak or see each other for three years, which was the best thing that could have happened to us. By putting my foot down and saying no to bullshit parenting, I moved on, lived my life to the fullest, and didn't take anything less than the respect that I deserved. I'm lucky that I had a support system in place for me when my dad wasn't there, but not everyone has that. Many LGBTQ+ kids have nobody to turn to and are kicked out to become homeless. Recognizing the privilege of my situation makes my involvement with the Trevor Project that much more of a personal necessity.

So, yeah, I'm gay as fuck. Have been since birth, and the moral of the story is I love it. If you don't, you can literally go. Homophobic people are outdated and life is too short to put up with them. My dad didn't get it immediately, but thanks to the time apart, he was able to grow up—something that may not have happened had I put up with his behavior. Nowadays, we both thank God I didn't.

high school
camp counselor

IF YOU WERE WATCHING ME FROM THE OUTSIDE, my walk to the principal's office may have seemed slow and calm, but I felt that I was about to shit myself. It was my senior year, and I was sure that this meeting was going to ruin my chances of graduating. There was no other explanation— I must have been found out, and I was finally going to be held accountable for my actions. How did I get into this mess, any-way?

It all started a week prior. I arrived at the middle school's parking lot at 6:00 a.m., bundled in winter gear from head to toe, with a duffel bag heaved over my shoulder. I was about to spend a week in a cabin with ten seventh graders, and I couldn't be more terrified. Every year, the entire seventh grade class of my school district went on a pilgrimage to Spring Hill, a camp-site up north in the middle of the woods. The district's high school seniors applied to be camp counselors for the event, and somehow I was chosen. I had no idea what I was getting myself into.

When I was a seventh grade camper, I was starstruck by my counselor. Since I was an aspiring drama club member, his being a leading male in the musicals and plays turned me to mush. Whatever he said went, and I was happy to follow his rules. Unfortunately, my own campers five years later were less than impressed with my ability to get bit parts in the plays and musicals. I was definitely going to have to work for their respect . . . or at least bribe them.

In preparation for our trip, we were given a list of things to pack—scarves, hats, gloves, the usual—but one thing stood out: candy. We were instructed to bring not too much and not too little. Just enough to make your campers think they'd got an edgy counselor. Campers themselves were forbidden to bring any candy to the camp, so it was the teachers' way of letting us be cool in the campers' eyes. Knowing my own pushover tendencies, and that most of the seventh graders were already my size if not taller, I knew I'd have to pack a *ton* of candy to get them to do what I said. The night before we left for the trip, I went to the grocery store and stocked up. As I wandered the candy aisle, I realized times had changed since I was a seventh grader. Like . . . caffeinated gum? I mean, sure, why not, but . . . really? I felt old and had no clue what the kids were into, so I just bought everything.

On the first day, we settled into our cabin, and my campers were already antsy. We had a bit of free time before the first activity, so I decided now was the time to assert my power and break out the goods. Before anything else, I laid down a few ground rules—no bragging to other campers about what I'd brought, and no eating anything outside of the cabin. Then, with each lanky prepubescent huddling around my luggage, I unzipped my bag and revealed the contraband. Gasps all around. Then they reached in and claimed what they could— from chocolates to gummies, sweets to extreme sours. I was their dealer, and they were hooked.

My campers rationed their candy supplies throughout the week, but they saved the majority of it for the final night. Taking place on the last night of camp, the dance was the biggest event of the week, and the sugar would help hype them up for it. After seven days of activities such as horseback riding, swimming, sledding, arts and crafts, and various games, the last evening was a chance to let loose. With a resident DJ blasting the hottest hits of 2006, campers stood around awkwardly, gathering the courage to approach each other. About thirty minutes into the event, the high school counselors were to make their grand entrance.

While we waited for our time to arrive, the rest of the camp counselors and I sat in the room adjacent to the dance hall. We were exhausted from the week we had all just endured. As we exchanged horror stories about our campers and their bizarre tendencies, I saw a few of the guys huddled near a snack table in the back. Never one to pass on free food, I got up and made my way over to them.

"Dude, you want some?" Jimmy Aikens asked. Jimmy was a super-popular guy who was involved in a lot of school activities. He was cool.

"Yeah, sure, totally," I replied. He handed me a quarter of

a brownie. I ate it in one swift bite, wondering, *Why so stingy?* Demonstrating how generosity should look, I helped myself to substantially more of the free food. With a full plate, I returned to the circle of counselors sharing horror stories. Jimmy tried to get my attention from the other side of the circle, mouthing something I couldn't quite understand. I tried to decipher his pointing at me and making a face with wide eyes, but I had no clue what he was going on about.

The camp advisers made their way into the room to let us know it was time. Throughout the week, the other counselors and I had rehearsed our grand-entrance routine, designed to wow the seventh graders. Clad in all pink and red clothes and accessories to go along with the Valentine's Day theme of the dance, we lined up behind the door.

Jimmy made his way over and looked me in the eyes, grinning. "Do you feel it yet?"

Before I could ask what he meant, the doors of the banquet hall swung open. This was our cue to run in, screaming and jumping to hype up the teenagers, with Sean Paul's "Temperature" as our sound track. As I leaped in the air, I started to feel a bit weird. Each leap felt more and more majestic, and the transition into "Buttons" by the Pussycat Dolls made me feel woozy and slow. I looked around and felt my neck swiveling incrementally, millimeter by millimeter, and my stomach dropped as I realized what was happening. Those were pot brownies.

Now, this wasn't my first time getting high, but it was definitely my first time high at a *seventh grade dance*. The first time I ever smoked pot was tenth grade, after a musical rehearsal. I was Cogsworth in our school's production of *Beauty and the Beast*, and one of the dishes from the "Be Our Guest" sequence thought we needed some bonding time, so we went to the mall, smoked a joint in the parking lot, and went to the food court to eat some Panda Express. I felt nothing, as it was my first time and I probably did it wrong.

The first time I ever *felt* high was with an upperclassman bad girl, Tiffani Miller. She wore heavy makeup and was a known party girl at my school and once you got to know her, she was incredibly kind, warm, and hilarious. We knew each other from Spanish class, and one day she asked me if I was into smoking. I lied and said yes because I didn't want to seem lame, and she invited me to come "chill" with her and her friends that night.

Tiffani lived near me, so I hurried over toward her house, which was a bit of a mess from the inside out. Tiffani may have been one of the nicest girls, but her life always seemed to be a bit disheveled. I was nervous and giddy, and when I made it to her front door, I texted her with my flip phone to let her know I had arrived.

On the other side of the door, I heard locks being unlocked and chains being unhooked until finally the door creaked open. She stuck her head out through the crack, eyes already glazed, and said calmly, "Excuse the shit everywhere." I laughed and assured her that I didn't care, and she opened the door.

As I stepped through the front door, I immediately realized she was not being figurative. Dog shit was everywhere, and her little Chihuahua circled my feet as I tiptoed among his droppings. I kept my cool, as if every house I visited had animal waste in the kitchen, and we made our way to the stairs leading up to her room. That night, I got way too high. We watched *Aqua Teen Hunger Force*, and we laughed for what felt like hours. I then walked home, fell asleep peacefully, and woke up feeling refreshed from a good night's rest. See how evil drugs can be sometimes?

I've since had plenty of good times with marijuana, and of course some bad times. The good times would be boring to tell you about, as it's typically me and some buddies watching *Sex and the City* and eating everything in the kitchen. The bad times are a little more interesting.

Once, my high school besties thought it would be a good idea to go see *X-Men 3* in the theater high out of our minds. It was packed, and we were in the back row. I was experiencing sensory overload and felt *very* nervous about mutants. As the previews began, I looked over at my friends, and they were so, so stoned. During one trailer, a huge boom sounded out of no-where. My best friend, Dolan, was so startled that he threw his full extra large bucket of popcorn into the air, and it showered the man in front of him. It was so mortifying that to this day he still brings it up every time we go to a movie.

The first time I combined alcohol and pot was just the worst. Please, if you're reading this, don't do it. While writing this, I googled if it had a name, and apparently it's called cross-fading? Listen, I had no idea what I was doing. All I know is that I was way too drunk and way too high, and I felt like I was going to shit out of every orifice of my body. I ended up having to run outside and lie in the snow because I was overheating.

Nowadays, I don't smoke often, but it's definitely far from the worst thing I could be doing with my evening. I'll do it with friends if I'm in the mood and with good people, but I never do it if I have to go in public. That's always where I've drawn the line. I like to be fully alert, aware, and in control of myself when I'm out and about, and substances—whether alcohol or marijuana—aren't the best for maintaining that control.

But my worst marijuana experience ever? It was at that seventh grade camp dance. If you read John Green's *The Fault in Our Stars*, you may recall a quote about a character falling in love "slowly, and then all at once." This was me, except instead of love, it was marijuana-induced paranoia. My main strategy was to stand at the perimeter of the dance, smiling and bopping my head, while repressing my terror. I briefly tried hiding in a bathroom stall, but I startled anytime someone came into the bathroom. What if they recognized my shoes? I sat on the toilet, legs straight out in front of me, questioning everything about my life.

I also spent what felt like a long time stirring the punch bowl. Out of the corner of my eye, I saw my campers approaching. They were extra-energetic, and when I asked if they were having fun, they all giggled conspiratorially. Obviously, I was too high to investigate further.

The worst moments of the night were when slow songs came on. Seventh graders lined up to slow-dance with the high school camp counselors they had crushes on. In the harsh and sober light of day, this dynamic is already dubious and unnerving. Stoned and with my paranoia reaching a crescendo, avoiding the eye contact of a lovelorn middle school tween while slow-dancing to Enrique Iglesias's "Hero"? There are no words.

The second the dance was over, I literally ran back to my

cabin and announced to my exhausted campers, "Lights out!" Thankfully, they were ready to crash, and as soon as my head hit the pillow, I was out. The next morning, we boarded the buses and made our way back home. We said our good-byes and I wished them well, praising God that my accidental high was never exposed.

The next week during one of my classes, my teacher received a call that interrupted his lesson. As he answered, his eyes went from staring off into space to snapping in my direction, and my stomach dropped. He put down the phone and said I needed to go to the office. The class went "OoooooooooOOOOO!" as the color left my face and I packed up my book bag. I made my way down the hall, ready to be expelled for my high-nanigans.

I waited in a chair as the secretary let the principal know I had arrived. After what felt like an eternity, the principal opened the door and solemnly told me to come inside. I walked in, sat in front of her desk, and prepared for the worst.

She started, "So last week at seventh grade camp—"

"I'm so sorry, I honestly didn't mean to!" I blurted out, on the brink of tears. I was so embarrassed and ashamed. I was ready for my punishment, knowing that this was going to be on my permanent record. I'd lose my job as a drive-thru specialist, I'd never go to college and become a fratguy who whips out his ruler, and I would probably end up living for the rest of my life in a run-down house smoking pot with dog shit all over my kitchen floor.

"Don't worry. We got a call from a parent this morning. I didn't even know what Jolt gum was?"

I looked up, puzzled.

"Apparently, he wants to sue the district because you gave his kid caffeinated gum. But honestly, it's sold in every grocery store and gas station in the candy aisle, you're fine. We just wanted to let you know about the situation."

I exhaled the biggest sigh of relief in my entire life. My future kitchen floor would be tasteful, immaculate, and 100 percent dog shit-free.

editor in grief

G OING INTO MY SENIOR YEAR OF HIGH SCHOOL, I felt the need for a change. Discussing options with my guidance counselor, I found two great ones: yearbook and journalism. Both classes set out to do the same thing: document the happenings of Okemos High School, one weekly, one annually. The two classes had some type of weird, historical, ongoing feud. With my need to fill two class slots, I decided to enroll in both, and as with a royal marriage to secure peace between two countries, I would end the war. I would bring harmony to my high school once again.

Both classes met separately before the school year started so we could familiarize ourselves with the other staff members. I soon realized that the classes couldn't have been more different. Journalism was full of hard workers and ambitious writers, all aggressively competing for stories to report on. Yearbook had a roster of uninspired dilettantes who picked straws to see who would be forced to work on the sports pages. The choice was obvious. I had found my tribe. I promptly dropped journalism before the first day of school.

As one of the unlucky few who had drawn the short straw, I was assigned the page for varsity football, and I was paired with Rachel Crouch, our editor in chief. To get ahead of our deadlines, yearbook staff took advantage of the fall sports teams having summer workout schedules, and we went to practices to take pictures before the school year even started. On a hot summer day, weeks before the start of school, I waited on my porch for Rachel to pick me up. I stepped into her car and shyly made small talk, having never spoken to her before in the past three years of high school together. In one afternoon of photographing hot and sweaty seniors in jerseys, we became best friends, and we were inseparable for the rest of the year. I had no clue that a year later, going our separate ways for college would inspire me to make my YouTube channel to keep in touch.

Yearbook had a new adviser that year, a Snow White look-alike with a high, squeaky voice. Still getting her bearings, she looked to the existing editor in chief for guidance. Displeased with having to teach the teacher, Rachel gave the school an ultimatum: either the teacher goes, or Rachel goes. Unfortunately for Rachel, they called her bluff, because obviously. With insider information about her impending departure, I applied for Rachel's position early, and I was appointed before anyone else on the staff even knew she was leaving. I had successfully executed the swiftest coup d'état the yearbook class had ever seen. History is written by the victors, and my pen and notepad were poised.

As the new editor in chief, I became obsessed with my role. I spent most of my free time editing layouts, writing copy, interviewing students and faculty, and attending events to document the 2006-7 school year properly. My most brilliant moments were when I abused my position of power to game the system, and by that I mean to get closer to boys.

It was pretty common knowledge at my school that I had an undying thirst for a tall, tan, muscular guy named Nick, who had the thickest caterpillar eyebrows. He was on the lacrosse team, and I was on cloud nine. I flirted with him playfully over the years, and while all of his bros thought it was hilarious, he took it in stride and laughed along, always kind and smiling. My adoration for Nick came to a culmination at the senior BBQ, an annual cookout in the school's courtyard. The intention was for the senior class to relax, unwind, and say their good-byes in their final week before graduation. As this event was one of my pages to cover for the yearbook, I circled the barbecue, snapping pictures of people who had yet to be featured much throughout the year.

When I saw Nick across the courtyard, I knew what I had to do: it was time to abuse my power and ask him for a picture. In recent years, I've mustered up the courage to walk up and ask people such as Harry Styles, Channing Tatum, and Joe Jonas for selfies, but back in high school, this was uncharted territory. We didn't even *call* them selfies. That word didn't even exist yet! While the event was full of my classmates embracing and posing for pictures all around us, I didn't have the balls to be so bold. Instead, I made up the most ridiculous lie.

"Hey, Nick. So . . . as you know, I'm editor of the yearbook, and it's really important to us that we get enough pictures of everyone, and this year, both of us have yet to be featured, so I'm sorry to ask, but we kind of have to do it." He looked at me puzzled. "My adviser is making us, we have to take a picture together. Right now, I'm afraid."

There it was. Not even a request. A mandate. Without waiting for a response, I awkwardly handed off the camera to another yearbook staff member, who looked at me wide-eyed. She shook her head slightly while gripping the camera, shooting a look that said both, "You know damn well you've put both of you in this fucking yearbook more than anyone else in the school" and "Say *cheese*."

Sorry, Nick. I'm also the reason why in the back of the yearbook, where parents buy ad space to write dedications for their graduating senior children, our dedications are placed next to each other. Listen, I was eighteen and a little crazy. I swear I won't do anything weird at our ten-year reunion (you *are* coming, right?).

My favorite staff member in yearbook class had to be Crystal Lynn. She would sign out the class's DSLR camera to go take new MySpace pictures in the closest bathroom. Her most iconic moment was while we were all frantically scrambling to meet a deadline, she broke the silence by screaming, *"Nobody move. I lost something."* All eyes darted her way as she slid forward off of her swivel desk chair and onto the floor. The yearbook adviser looked at me in shock, and I rolled my eyes, unfazed by Crystal's antics. After a moment of crawling on the carpet beneath the table, she poked her head back up and groaned, "Has anyone seen my tongue ring?" *This* girl was in charge of preserving my generation's high school memories. Sorry, Okemos High School, class of 2007.

One of my favorite things about being yearbook editor in chief was being able to use excuses like "Sorry, I have to go take pictures of custodians" if I ever had to get out of something or go hook up with a guy. In the second semester of senior year, it was mostly the latter, with a straight guy I had known since middle school. Not until that year did we run into each other at a party, refilling our drinks upstairs alone in the kitchen, and end up making out in the backyard underneath the porch. From then on, I was over at his place every day after school, until finally we decided we couldn't wait until after school, and we began to meet during sixth hour, which was when I had yearbook class.

We'd text each other ten-minute warnings, excuse ourselves from our respective classrooms, approach the fine-arts wing from different hallways, and meet furtively in front of the choir-room door. After lunch, the choir room was empty, and I knew the trick to opening it without a key: a small wiggle and quick thrust. In the privacy of the choir room, I repeated this same maneuver on him, which kept him coming back most days for the rest of the school year. I'd then scurry back to the yearbook computer lab and oversell just *how great the shots I just got* were, a little too pleased with my own pun.

In between the glorified scrapbooking we staff did during yearbook class, we spent most of our time browsing the Internet. These were the days before Twitter, Tumblr, and Instagram, but I remember a life-changing event that happened one day in February during that sixth-hour class. I was nearing a deadline, working hard to finalize a page, and out of the corner of my eye I saw the entire staff huddled around one computer. Before I could insist they get back to work, they burst into laughter, and I had to see what all the fuss was about.

"What . . . is happening?" I asked, peeking over shoulders at a video of a man in a wig, screaming, *Fuck you,* with interludes of a woman dancing with a flaming hula hoop.

"Wait, wait, don't look yet!" my classmates insisted, saying I had to watch it from the beginning. I did, and thus was my first viewing of one of the first viral videos of the Internet, "Shoes."

"What TV show was this on?" I asked, bewildered, after watching it in full.

"None, this guy just uploaded it to YouTube," my classmate replied. "He's got other videos too."

Prior to this, I had always thought of YouTube as a place for people to upload class projects or family videos, with the occasional "fail" or "cat" video. But this guy uploaded his work? And people subscribed to find out what he'd upload next? It was so foreign to me. I went back to my desk to continue with the yearbook, but couldn't get the beat of "Shoes" out of my head. Over the next few months, I wrapped up the documentation of our life in high school through yearbook class, and then I slowly fell down the rabbit hole of finding other content creators on YouTube. I had no clue that this was about to become my life.

Side note: while writing this book, a high school yearbook editor in chief emailed me asking if I wanted to buy an ad for their yearbook. Knowing just how hard it is to sell to sponsors, I decided to pay it forward and purchase a full page. Check it out below, maybe it'll speak to you if you're approaching your own graduation.

Hi Utica High School!

My name is Tyler Oakley, and when I first got the email from Vita Simmons about buying an ad in the yearbook, I was like YAAAS, SLAY ME! Mainly because I used to be Editor-In-Chief of my own high school's yearbook (SHOUTOUT to Okemos High!), so I know how hard it is to sell ads. Plus, an opportunity to shamelessly self promote? Why not!

So I figured we'd have a little heart-to-heart, just us girls.

Here's the thing - back in high school. I thought every audition, every test, every interaction... was the end of the world. Chill. It will be okay. Yes, do your best, but know that a college rejection is not the end of the world, or your voice cracking during a solo will not kill you.

I spent so much time worried about what everyone else thought about me that I didn't realize... nobody cares! Everyone around me was freaking out too. Sure there will be some rude people, but spoiler alert, they're probably going to peak in high school.

You will soon look back at your time at Utica High and wonder how it went by so quick - so take it all in now. Try out for the play, say hello to the people you want to be friends with, enjoy yourself, have fun. This is all just a little reminder. Okay, I'mma go. I'll see you on the Internet.

♥ Tyler Oakley

thtory of my life

E VEN AT A YOUNG AGE, I HAD A PROFOUND dis-
taste for offensive stereotypes. This quality inadver-
tently led me to an obsession with a kids' book series
called the Adventures of the Bailey School Kids. In the fifty-
one-book series (!), the four main characters navigate their
world and find mythical creatures breaking the mold and defy-
ing harmful stereotypes.

With such titles as *Bigfoot Doesn't Square Dance*, *Witches
Don't Do Back Flips*, *Angels Don't Know Karate*, and *Wolfmen
Don't Hula Dance*, I was exposed to progressive, socially conscious literature that *finally* exposed humans for what I sus-
pected they were: offensive and prejudiced, even when it came
to creatures that didn't exist. I was appalled.

Growing up gay, I too was subjected to endless stereotyp-
ing, and like the titles of the books I read as a child, I was ready
to break the mold and teach my classmates a thing or two
about what it meant to be queer. You think all gays have a great
sense of style? *Ha!* I'll show you! Introducing the Bailey School

Kids' latest, *Gays Don't Have Bad Style*—the unexpected tale of a twelve-year-old me with a bowl cut parted down the middle, sporting an Old Navy Tech Vest, paired with socks and sandals, single-handedly proving the cliché wrong.

Figuring out who I was in the world wasn't the easiest. Although I had plenty of representation when it came to being white, male, and cisgender (the opposite of transgender), my sexuality as reflected in pop culture usually boiled down to stereotypical gay characters. Typically sidekicks or the gay best friend, and for whom being gay was their defining attribute. They styled hair, gave makeovers, lisped, and were generally prissy and whimsical. And though being gay I felt underrepresented, I can't imagine what it would have been like identifying as lesbian, bisexual, or transgender—I may have gotten the bare minimum of a poor representation, but those groups had virtually none at all.

When I did see those gay characters, I also saw the ridicule they received, both in the shows themselves and from the people in my own life making comments. I learned quickly that a lot of the world was bothered by their very existence as homosexuals, and that displaying the stereotypical attributes of a gay person was not something to be celebrated. Minimization and blending in seemed to be a gay person's safest route.

Luckily, my close friends, family, and the majority of my high school couldn't care less about gender identity or sexual orientation. I was taught that being myself was not only okay, but encouraged—and by being unapologetically yourself, you thrive and inspire others to thrive. I guess that was why I created my own YouTube channel—as a place for me to be unapologetically genuine, and to express myself despite how any-one else might view me, or what people might say about me.

Being on YouTube, though, exposed me to a much larger population, and I was subjected to opinions outside the circle of my close friends, family, and community. By now, I've read every nasty thing a person can say about someone else—all di-rected at me. One of the strangest things I've read was that I embellish my stereotypically gay mannerisms for more views or attention. While I do enjoy a good marketing strategy, this couldn't be any further from the truth.

One day, I read a criticism of myself aloud to my friend Korey. I went through a list of all the faults this person found in me. Arrogant, self-centered, blah blah blah . . . the usual, nor-mal complaints. Hey, if I weren't self-centered, I wouldn't have a YouTube channel. Do you think any well-adjusted person would ever think to self-produce a broadcast of his own face to the entire world? Who *does* that? But then . . . I saw it—the final criticism, an accusation that simply went too far: for views, I faked having a lisp.

"Can you believe that? Let's start with the fact that I don't even *have* a lisp."

Korey's brow furrowed as he glanced in my direction. With a tilt of the head, he asked, "Are you being serious?"

"What do you mean? Of course I'm being serious. Are *you* being serious?"

"Don't tell me you don't know that you have a lisp . . ."

Wait. This was dire. It's not that I have a problem with lisps, it's just that I never thought I had one. It's like when I was in sixth grade and this kid told me in the hot-lunch line that I had a hook head. When I asked what that even meant, he said that the back of my head jutted out like a pirate's hook, like I've got a big brain or at least a sizable tumor going on. I had no clue whether it was true, but he had planted the seed of doubt in my big hook head. To this day, you will *never* catch me profiling my silhouette.

But back to the alleged lisp! I couldn't believe that with years of filming myself and editing my own videos, I could have even subconsciously chosen to ignore the defect in my voice. Even before I made videos, I had spent much of my childhood calling our local radio station, K105.3 FM, every morning on the way to school, to request songs just to hear myself on the radio. Could I have been so repressed that I ignored every broadcast of my own voice? Then again, "Tubthumping" by Chumbawamba doesn't have an *s* in it, so who knows . . . maybe if I'd been requesting the Thpice Girls, I would have heard it?

Or consider the time when I spent an entire five-hour drive on a family trip to a theme park in Ohio memorizing Alanis Morissette's classic "Ironic." This laid the groundwork to record my own cover on a cassette tape in the sound booth for $5. Surely, if I was developing a lisp back in 1996, I would have heard it in my vocal stylings of Alanis's lyrics? Yet, despite my own flawless, pitch-perfect vocals in my headphones, I don't recall ever detecting any hint of a speech impediment in the recording. Isn't *that* ironic?

I've heard it said that if you were to run into yourself on the street, you wouldn't even recognize that it's you because your self-perception is so distorted from what others see. Maybe the same is to be said about our own voices. Fearing the worst, I did what any levelheaded, potentially self-loathing gay would do—I sent an emergency text to my friend Millie, who was a speech-pathology major, telling her I needed to see her immediately, in perthon.

Millie and I had been friends for a while, and she never once brought up my alleged issue. In hindsight, maybe she was just being polite? In the same way that if you've got a friend with a lazy eye, you don't mention it because they must know already? Actually, I'll be right back. Let me find a mirror.

Okay, I'm back, I don't think I have a lazy eye. Which is good, because I sat down with Millie on that fateful day and forced her to look me dead in the eyes—both of them, at the same time—and tell me the *truth*.

"So . . . is it true? What they say about me?" I prompted dramatically. "Do I have a lisp?"

Millie looked at me long and hard. "Yes."

She began to explain the mechanics of the condition, but my mind wandered and her words became muffled in the background. My worst fears that I'd never considered had suddenly been realized. Was this it? I thurely wath not a pothethor of a lithp—I would have known by now? Someone would have told me. Do I have no real friends? Has my entire life been a lie?

I cut her off. "Maybe it's just an extended *s*?"

"Yeah, no." Millie said bluntly, as if to shut down my bargaining stage of grief. "Are you self-conscious about it?"

"No! Obviously not. Why would I be?" I snapped. But was I?

Days went by, and it was the only thing I could think about. When asked if I wanted milk with my grande iced coffee, my request for a little bit of thoy milk became an issue. Requesting Lady Gaga's "Applauthe" at the local gay bar was a whammy, as well.

I slowly began to realize that maybe I *was* self-conscious about it. Sure, I was obviously openly gay, and I had been for over a decade, but was my refusal to accept my speech imped-iment something deeper than a lack of self-awareness? A hint of some type of self-loathing, internalized homophobia caused by a culture that taught minorities that if they wanted to be ac-cepted, they had to blend in? That they must be straight acting, normal sounding, not wearing anything that makes them stand out *too* much? Was my *refusal* to acknowledge my lisp—even when brought to my attention—a conscious, last-ditch effort to tell myself that I had been blending in all along?

So what if I did have a lisp? Some people do fit some ste-reotypes. Is that going to be the end of the world? In every community, some people will fit every stereotype, and some people will fit no stereotypes, and both are valid representa-tions for that community. No one person can be the end-all representation, and expecting any one person to represent a huge group of people puts them on a dubious pedestal and likely to be toppled.

So maybe the moral of *Witches Don't Do Back Flips* only applies to some witches, and that's okay. Maybe finding exam-ples of people who break stereotypes doesn't erase the exis-tence of those who fit them. Because obviously, some gays have lisps, and some don't, and fitting that stereotype isn't good or bad, it just is.

Being a part of a community isn't about being or even

avoiding being society's preconception of that community. It's about trying to be your best self, whoever you are. I in no way think I am "the voice" of any community; all I can do is try to be a voice and show people that they can also be a voice. I fit some stereotypes, I don't fit others. And that's okay. I'll never be a gay that every other gay can relate to, but if by being myself, lisp included, I'm a gay that one lonely twelve-year-old gay in the Middle of Nowhere, with his parted bowl cut and inadvisable zip-up vest, can identify with and thus feel less alone, then I've done my job. And that makes me feel fantathtic.

the one that got away

"I THINK I MIGHT NOT BE STRAIGHT," Adam said.

Smiling and tilting my head, I looked up from my Scrabble letters and into his hazel eyes. Hazel is how you describe the color of someone's brown eyes when you're in love. Hazel is the dreamy kind of shit-colored you could get lost in forever. "Oh?"

I could see the weight lifting off his shoulders, as if now, having said those words out loud, he was finally, literally unburdened. This is no surprise—that's typically the feeling gay people experience once they come to terms with their sexuality. For me, the surprise came instead from the fact that he was saying these words to his boyfriend of six months. But I guess I'm getting ahead of myself. Let me start at the beginning.

"I'm straight," Adam said.

Frowning and *not* tilting my head, I looked up from my computer screen. *Who does this twink think he's fooling?* I thought.

"Oh?" I replied. I turned to our two female coworkers and gave them knowing looks.

They grinned, convinced that they had found for themselves a straight, eligible, athletic, charming guy with ambition and the perfect amount of chest hair (judging by his Facebook pictures, which all three of us had already stalked). "Told you," one of them whispered, as she put her headset back on.

I rolled my eyes and returned to my shift as a telemarketer, my relatively new job of calling alumni to ask them to donate money to the university. As I dialed my phone, I spaced out. I was distracted and annoyed that the one guy I had a crush on at work identified as straight. There's nothing worse than sitting across from a charming, hot, straight boy. *Nothing.* Except maybe being a telemarketer.

After my shift, I walked home bundled up against the cold, shuffling across campus back to my dorm room. I thought about Adam. From the little curls in his hair, to his dumb, monotone voice, to the arch of his eyebrow when he'd tease me and my coworkers, to his brown eyes that were almost more of a hazel? This boy was cute.

As the semester went on, Adam became my work bestie, the person with whom I shared most of my inside jokes and sideways glances. In between calls, we'd lean over the divider separating our adjacent cubicles to eavesdrop and distract the others from their work. Despite his tragic sexual orientation, we treated each other like work boyfriends. Yet, despite their surprisingly transparent efforts, none of our female coworkers surrounding us seemed to be exactly his type. His charm attracted them into constant orbit, but his attention always wandered back to me.

"He's beeeeeeeeeeautiful," sighed my best friend, Ilana. I had just spent a full minute scrolling through Adam's Facebook profile pictures, before deciding the perfect one to show her.

"Right?! And he says he's straight, but he's so playful with me, and I don't know, it's just, like, why would he give me so much attention if he was straight? Also, he's in ski club, and how cute is that?"

"That's great and all, but is he Jewish?" Ilana was in the market for a nice Jewish husband. I could relate because my first boyfriend in high school introduced me to the culture, and ever since, I always dreamed of someday having a Jewish mother-in-law.

"I don't think so?"

"Well, feel free to invite him on Monday, regardless."

Due to the school's colors (green and white) and obsession with drinking, one of the biggest holidays at Michigan State University was, not surprisingly, St. Patrick's Day. Between drinking green beers and green Jell-O shots and green vodka, all while wearing green wigs and hats and shirts and leggings, MSU did St. Patty right, and this Monday would be no exception.

Because it was a holiday, Ilana and I decided to branch out from our typical plans of partying in the dorms to attending a real-life frat party. I knew no men in frats, so obviously we went Ilana's route, and we prepared to attend the Jewish fraternity's annual St. Patrick's Day party. What if I met someone? What if I met . . . *the* one? I could see it now: we'd all be sitting in the dark, wood-paneled, strangely musty basement, chasing our Popov shots with cherry Smirnoff sips, complaining about professors and asking each other our majors, when all of a sudden, he'd arrive. The one. We'd fall in love, and his parents would like me more than him, and we'd fight over who had to lint-roll the couch after I let our golden retriever lie on it from time to time, and we'd grow old together, all because of one chance encounter in a Jewish fraternity's drunken celebration of an Irish saint. A quintessentially American love story.

After the next day's classes, I went into work, sat down, and logged in to get started with my calls.

Before the first ring, up popped Adam, practically jumping out of his cubicle, wide-eyed and grinning. "Hey, boy. Whatcha doin' on St. Patrick's Day?"

I held up a finger as the alumna on the other side of the call answered. I went into my memorized script as Adam slumped down, leaning onto the divider, never breaking eye contact, making faces at me with his head resting on his folded arms. The boy was going to be the death of me.

Adam's eyes widened as he began to hear the surprisingly high volume blasting from my headset, as the alumna screamed at the top of her lungs, demanding to know if I appreciated how much student debt she was still in. As I tried to talk her down, I was cut off midsentence by a dial tone. She was done with me, and I could get back to Adam. "I'm going to the Jewish frat. They're having a big party. Will you be around?"

"Yes. Let's pregame at your place," Adam suggested with a smirk as he picked up my long-outdated flip phone, glanced back and forth between it and me, clearly judging both phone and owner, before putting his number into my address book. Well now, it seems a *boy* just *gave* me *his* number. I was so heart-eyes emoji, and this was before the heart-eyes emoji even existed. Monday night couldn't come quickly enough.

As I meticulously adjusted the objects on my dorm-room desk just so, as to appear both effortlessly organized and yet lived-in, I heard a knock on the door. Decked out in all green, I leaped toward the door, eager for my night to begin. With his flipped hair and a huge grin, Adam bounced into the room. His mono-tone voice seemed especially silly as he attempted enthusiasm, yelling, "Yaaaaaaaaaay."

We did shots until we heard another knock, and Ilana peeked into the room. As she hugged Adam hello for the first time, she looked at me over his shoulder, and her wide eyes communicated her approval. *Adorable,* she mouthed. *I know,* I mouthed in reply. The three of us continued to drink for a bit, then—clad in all green—we made our way downstairs and hailed a cab.

We pulled up to a broken-down mansion, vibrating from the loud music playing inside. This was the home of the Jewish fraternity, so we made our way through the crowd. Ilana knew the mother of every Jewish boy in the frat, so we had the VIP status to skip the line and make our way to the beer keg.

"So what's your type?" Ilana yelled, asking Adam between gulps of beer, nudging me and with her eyes saying to me, *I'm asking for you, if you couldn't tell. Hopefully he says boys with glasses and a pathological need for attention.* Yes, her eyes said all of that.

"I'm not sure . . . I'll know when I see her."

Oh, so we're gonna play *that* game still? Okay, well, if you're identifying as straight for the night, I'm identifying as straight-to-bed, because daddy needs dick and he's gonna find some, regardless of whether it's you, Adam.

Adam and I slumped onto a couch in the basement and did a "Cheers" with our drinks, but my real attention was on scanning the crowd for Mr. Right (Now). The scene was exactly as I'd imagined, wood-paneled walls and a musty aura—except my soul mate didn't seem to be walking down those stairs. I turned to Adam, annoyed, and made conversation.

We told each other our majors and complained about professors. Eventually, we both concluded that we had gotten a little too drunk prematurely, and we were nearing blackout. We agreed that we should probably make our way back toward the dorms and call it a night. I sighed as I walked up the stairs, admitting defeat as we made our way outside to hail a cab.

We climbed into the backseat, Adam scooting all the way over and me following in after him. I leaned forward to slur to the driver, "We'll be making . . . uhhh, two stops pleasssssse. Wilsssson Hall, first." As I leaned back against the seat, my arms braced at my sides, holding me up. I closed my eyes and felt myself almost spinning. Maybe all that alcohol wasn't my smartest move.

Frustrated and beating myself up over my failed tactic of finding a boyfriend at the party, I decided, *Fuck this, I'm done searching for a guy. If a guy wants me, that's his choice. I need to chill the fuck out and just enjoy life, and that's when someone's going to come along and sweep me off my feet.*

My head spun, I closed my eyes, and I began to drift off to sleep. Suddenly, my eyes shot open and I snapped back to sober reality.

I looked down between Adam and me. What I thought might be happening was indeed confirmed to be happening. Adam's hand had slid its way under mine, palm down, so that I was now holding it between us. I looked to my left and saw his eyes were closed. Was this an accident? Did he forget I was a guy? *What's happening?*

Just to test the waters, I gave his hand the softest squeeze, and he flipped his hand around, palm up, to hold mine. *This can't be happening.* I closed my eyes again as his fingers slowly interlaced with mine, his thumb gliding over my palm. I opened my eyes again and looked in his direction. He was already looking my way, smiling. *This isn't happening.* I smiled back. Without a word, he scooted his body slowly my direction, never breaking eye contact, until his face hovered an inch away from mine. *Yep, those eyes are definitely hazel.*

"Hi," I whispered.

"Hey," he whispered back, grinning.

I melted, and with that, he leaned toward me, closing the gap. His kiss was full, and his hands were ambitious, and he only pulled away for a second to make one request.

"Driver, please make that *one* stop."

When I'm hungover, I usually wake up uncomfortably early, head pounding and unable to fall back to sleep. This morning, my hand involuntarily smacked my forehead, cooling it and shielding my eyes from the sun beginning to blaze through the blinds of my window. I groaned quietly as I peeked through one eye. It was no dream: there he was.

It was March 18, and I couldn't believe the previous night had actually happened. Chin up, mouth agape, eyes closed, and completely naked, Adam was sprawled across my bed. This wasn't happening. I mean, it was, thank God, but how did it happen? I closed my eyes again and began to piece together the night before, a jigsaw with missing pieces and no discernible borders.

I had a vague memory of crashing into the elevator of my dorm, tangling into each other as soon as the door shut, half-sloppily making out and half-giggling uninhibitedly. Another vague memory of crashing into my dorm room, interrupting my roommate and his girlfriend, who were celebrating the holiday in their own way on the top bunk. I covered my eyes with my hands and told them not to go, not to let us interrupt their fun, that we'd be quiet. As if my sober roommate from Texas and his girlfriend wouldn't mind some gay bottom-bunk rocking in tandem with that of their top bunk. Angrily, they leaped down from the top bunk, storming out with their blankets—heading somewhere I couldn't care less about, as Adam and I laughed and fell into my own bed. Then it hit me in a flash what had happened next.

Now, the next day, I carefully turned my body and angled myself toward him. There he was, the prize possession of telemarketing, soundly snoring in my bunk bed. It's crazy how the carefree and ravenous things you can do with someone at two in the morning can make complete sense at the time, but in the glow of dawn just five hours later, they unspool a skein of questions and implications. How drunk were we? Surely we both were consenting adults, but with alcohol involved, was he going to freak out waking up with a man? Will we even speak to each other tomorrow at work? Was it his first time, as well as mine?

Head pounding, I slipped out from under the covers and tiptoed to the bathroom as quietly as I could. I peed, brushed my teeth, washed my face, drank a glass of water, took two Advil, and looked in the mirror. Holy shit. Last night actually happened. I looked at my reflection and laughed under my breath at the ridiculousness of the situation. I was still unable to believe that the guy I had a crush on was in my bed. Through the pain of my hangover, I grinned.

Intending to sneak back into my sheets, I delicately opened the bathroom door and was surprised to see Adam, clothed, on the edge of my bed and tying his shoelaces.

I broke the silence. "Good morning . . . how are you feeling? Crazy night, no?"

"Yeah, the party was fun, thanks for letting me tag along," Adam replied nonchalantly. As if the most eventful part of our evening happened at the Jewish frat party. I froze in my tracks and looked at him, puzzled. Was he going to act like nothing had happened?

"Hey, uh, thanks for letting me crash, I should probably get going." He never met my eyes. I'd never seen anybody take such intense interest in his shoelaces.

"Oh, yeah, no problem," I said as he stood up. "You sure you have to go so soon?" I offered the glass of water I had poured for him, but he slipped past me.

"I'll see you at work," he said, already halfway out the door. And just like that, he was gone.

Holding two full glasses of water, I stood for a long time in my underwear, in the middle of my dorm room.

"What the fuck *was* last night?" my roommate, David, asked. We were paired for cohabitation randomly by the school, but we got along surprisingly well. He was from Texas, and when we first found each other on Facebook and exchanged information, he terrified me. We talked on instant messenger, where he revealed that, for fun, he and his friends surfed—pulled by a truck—in the muddy trenches on the sides of roads in Houston, Texas, after it rained. I was sure that I would be rejected as soon as he realized that, for fun, me and my friends sucked dick, rain or shine.

But he turned out to be great. Sure, we had our differences, but he respected me and my lifestyle, as I did his. One of the strange things about going through the different stages in your life as a gay man is that you experience coming out over and over. I had been out for more than five years, and I was comfortable in my skin, but going off to college and having a stranger as my roommate made me relive the entire process.

I came out to David one night at 2:00 a.m., after returning from a dorm party full of liquid courage. He was up on his top bunk watching *Planet Earth* when I stormed in and wasted no time word-vomiting my confession: *"David, I need to tell you something I'm gay but that doesn't mean I'm going to try to have sex with you or anything I just need you to know because it's just who I am I can't help it, I was born—"*

"Dude, obviously, I know." He chuckled, pausing *Planet Earth*. "Is that all?"

Coming out always feels like it's going to be a bigger deal than it ever ends up being. "Yeah, I guess."

"What time is your first class tomorrow? We should figure out our showering schedule." Just like that, he had moved on to more important things, like clocks and grout. Here's a picture of when I ran into him one night at the Whiskey Barrel Saloon, a line-dancing and mechanical-bull bar. Behind us, you'll see Rachel and Dolan, my two friends from high school that I made my YouTube channel to keep in touch with.

But let's go back to March 18. I was sprawled out, still recovering from my hangover. I looked over toward David's desk, where he had been hunched over studying. As a mechanical-engineering student, he was always studying. As a communications student, I was always in bed struggling through a hangover. This was us in a snapshot.

"I don't know what last night was. It was so spur-of-the-moment and out-of-the-blue, and Adam's *straight*, or at least he says he is."

"Okay, well, he's not straight. If he was straight, he wouldn't have slept with you."

Well, that was a fair point. My flip phone vibrated.

"He just texted me," I squawked.

Hey you. Wanna grab dinner tonight?

"What do I say?!"

"Well, do you want to get dinner with him or not? That's your answer." Again, structurally sound.

I said yes. Then, after waiting for hours to pass that felt like an eternity, the time came for our date. I made my way down the hall and waited in line outside my dorm's cafeteria entrance, tapping my wallet in my pocket in anticipation. As I neared the entrance, I scanned the tables.

There he sat, looking down, tapping away at his BlackBerry—his brown hair flipped effortlessly, his stubble just the right length. He was so put together, and I felt so disheveled. I still couldn't believe the night I'd had with him. I blushed just thinking about it.

"ID please?" the cafeteria worker asked. I broke my longing gaze and fumbled for my wallet, just as my phone started vibrating in my other pocket. I fished that out too, and three words lit up on my screen: *I see you.*

I glanced in his direction and was struck by his gaze; his eyes met mine, and he perched his chin on the palm of his hand. He had the slightest smile. *This boy is going to wreck me.*

In between scoops of Chinese orange chicken and white rice, we talked about everything except the night before—his estrangement from his mom, the clubs I was in during high school, his hobby of refurbishing furniture, my fondness for Scrabble, his adoration of Céline Dion's greatest-hits album, my love of wraparound porches—everything, everything except what had happened the last night. I didn't want to scare him off by bringing it up, but I also couldn't go on pretending that it didn't happen or that it wasn't a big deal for me.

"So about last night . . . ," I started.

"Listen . . . I'm sorry I ran out this morning. I was planning on acting like I was too drunk to remember what happened, but that wouldn't be fair. It was just a lot." He lowered his voice. "I'm straight, though. You know that, right?"

"Right, of course. Let's go back to talking about *Céline's greatest hits*."

He didn't so much as smirk.

"Will you hand me my phone? It's on my desk," I whispered, pointing. David Archuleta, *American Idol*'s adorable Mormon Monchhichi look-alike, was up next to perform "Angels" by Robbie Williams, for Inspirational Music week. I was ready to be moved to tears. Adam handed me my flip phone, so I could prepare to vote via text for as long as was allowed.

It had been twenty-four days since St. Patrick's Day, and since then, *American Idol* nights had become our thing. Adam would come over twice a week for dinner in my building's cafeteria, we'd watch Paula Abdul flounce for an hour, and then we'd vote while chatting about anything and everything. I'd always vote for David Archuleta: Adam would vote for whoever he thought was best that week. Such a fair-weather fan. We didn't call our *American Idol* nights dates, but they did include a meal, a social activity, and an adult activity—so if we were to continue with no labels, I was 100 percent fine with that.

As Ryan Seacrest was about to introduce David Archuleta, I shushed Adam authoritatively, despite that he wasn't talking. Adam's phone began vibrating, and I glared at him with a look that said, *If you are taking this call, you are taking it in the hallway—DAVID ARCHULETA IS ABOUT TO SING.*

"I should take this," he whispered. He leaned in to kiss my neck before scurrying out of the room. If a kiss was involved, I guess one interruption was allowed.

David Archuleta was slowly circled in a wide-angle camera shot, which then zoomed in on his adorable, lovable face. His voice quivered as he sang and played the grand piano center stage. Thirty seconds into his rendition of "Angels," I was already crying. There was just something about this guy. It could also have been the song—a cherubic boy with a heavenly voice was singing something so sweet and tender. It was all too much for me.

Halfway through the performance, Adam reappeared. I shushed him again, even though he had been completely silent. He leaned against the doorway and watched the performance, holding his phone to his ear. Even Adam, who was usually a steel trap emotionally, had tears in his eyes. Behold the power of David Archuleta.

Thunderous applause, a heavy sigh from me, and *American Idol* cut to commercial. I turned my head and asked who called.

"That was my dad. My mom is dead."

If I had to pinpoint the exact moment when Adam was ready to stop the charade and accept that we cared about each other—and that we might have a future—it was that night. It was the first time he invited me to his dorm room, the first time we cuddled instead of fucked, the first time I saw him cry, and the first time I didn't deflect with humor. We were stuck there, in that moment, with only each other. For the first time, we were unafraid to lean on each other.

When someone you care about suffers a devastating loss, there isn't much you can say. In almost any situation, I typically give honest, blunt advice. A friend stole your man? Set her front lawn on fire. Your roommate doesn't wash his dishes? Shatter those dishes and delicately lay them under his sheets. Can't decide which shirt to buy? Buy both and a third, because American Apparel gives you a discount if you purchase three of any item. Mom dies? I've got nothing. This was one of the first times I was left speechless, and I felt like I was speechless for weeks. What I did know to do was to hug him more than he'd ever ask for—so that's what I did.

"Thank you for being so . . . there," Adam said, putting his hand on my leg. He always drove, I always sat in the passenger seat. We'd been seeing each other for a few months now, and we had developed our little ways. His hand on my knee was one of them.

"You would do the same for me," I said. I brought his hand up to my lips and kissed his fingers softly. I thought about what I was dying to say out loud but was too terrified to reveal. Something I'd never been quite sure of before with anyone else, but was so undeniably positive I was feeling now: *I loved him.*

With our first year of university coming to a close, we said our good-byes. Adam packed up his dorm room into his SUV. As he lifted each box, his lean, muscular arms flexed, and I melted. As he reached up to close the trunk, his T-shirt rose and exposed his tan, hairy midriff. I stood on the sidewalk, arms folded, frowning melodramatically. The weight of separation felt so heavy.

"Fourth of July isn't that far away," he said, as we walked back into his dorm's empty hallway. Most of the people on his floor had already moved out, and his need to hide his affection for me wasn't in the forefront of his mind. As I stepped into his empty room, I heard him close the door behind me. I looked out his window at the parents helping their kids pack up their stuff in the parking lot below. "I can't wait to watch the fireworks with you," he whispered into my ear, and he wrapped his arms around me.

I was staying in the dorms as a sports-camp counselor that summer, and Adam was heading back to the Upper Peninsula of Michigan, where he was from. He'd invited me to come up to his hometown for a few days for the Fourth of July, and it would be my first trip to the Upper Peninsula.

Leading up to the trip, time seemed to stand still. I counted down the days by crossing them off on the calendar I kept fixed to my door.

After what felt like an eternity of waiting, I packed up my car and started my road trip. I was speeding so much that I got pulled over twice within hours. The first time, the police officer simply gave me a ticket. The second cop asked when the last time I got pulled over was, and when I replied, "Today," he began screaming at me about how I'd more likely die than reach my destination.

I pocketed the tickets and viewed them as fees I was happy to pay to see my boyfriend sooner. I arrived way ahead of schedule.

During that trip, I played the role of Adam's "college buddy" here to visit for the holiday. The charade was sometimes thrilling but always frustrating. I felt so close to him in private, but in public he virtually looked through me. If I'd known better then, I wouldn't have developed a relationship like that. The little things kept me hooked, though.

He showed his intimacy in small ways, just for us. When his dad asked one night during dinner if Adam had a girlfriend, he smirked at me with a devilish grin. I was his dirty little secret. Under the table, I ran my foot up his leg to stake my claim.

One day, we took a hike through Marquette's woods to a local landmark, the Blackrocks. It's a cliff overlooking Lake Superior where brave locals jump off and free-fall into the numbingly cold water. We wore our swimsuits, just in case the water was tolerable, but the unpopulated cliff indicated that it was way too cold for anyone today. One dip of a toe in the water confirmed that there was no way I'd be voluntarily taking the leap. So, of course, Adam elected the involuntary route. While I was looking out at the water from the edge of the cliff, Adam took a running start behind me, grabbed me around the waist, and leaped. The two of us fell, screaming, until we hit the impossibly cold water below. Gasping for air, I swore I could kill him, but before I could even begin to yell, he wrapped himself around me and kissed me, deep, long, and full. I barely remembered that I couldn't breathe. I swam to the edge, climbed out of the water, and stomped up the hill. I was soaked, freezing, and out of breath, but also grinning ear to ear.

We spent Independence Day itself adventuring through his town. While walking from his house to the Fourth of July parade, we took a detour through a neighborhood of cobblestone streets and houses with large wraparound porches. Young, dumb, and infatuated, we talked about what kind of dogs we'd want when we became grown-ups or if we wanted kids someday. Golden retriever, multiple kids, perfect. We walked past a few toddlers playing in a front lawn, and he leaned over and said, "You're gonna be a good dad." This was my version of talking dirty.

That night, we threw on a couple sweaters and made our way to one of Marquette's other landmarks, the ore docks, where the city launched fireworks over the lake. We sat on the large rocks on the edge of the lake as the show began, watching the sky illuminate. "I love you," Adam whispered into my ear. I melted.

After that weekend, I made my way back to the dorms, absolutely head over heels in love. I had months to go until school started and I would see him again, but in the meantime, I was beyond smitten, reeling. Never before had I felt this.

While a lot of my time that summer was spent working with the visiting sports campers, the rest was spent waiting for Adam's calls or texts. One way I kept occupied was by watching seasons of *Grey's Anatomy* and living vicariously through the doctors and their love affairs. That summer, everything spoke to me and everything reminded me of Adam. The sound track to *Grey's Anatomy*, especially, took over my brain, and one song in particular embodied how I felt about Adam: "Part of the beauty of falling in love with you is the fear you won't fall."

I had Joshua Radin's "The Fear You Won't Fall" on repeat. While I now look back and cringe, I even made a music-video montage of me looking pensive in different spots of our university's botanical garden. Graciously, Adam called it cute, but looking back, I was *crazy*. I couldn't help it. I blame love.

"How many people here are in a relationship with someone else in the class?"

Hands flew up by the pair, the lovebirds glancing at each other, giddy.

"By the time you finish this course, almost all of you will have broken up." As if shot from the air, the hands dropped, and the lecture began.

It was fall semester of my sophomore year, and I was in COM225, a course at Michigan State University about relationships and love—taught by a married couple. I would enroll in plenty of classes by Steve and Kelly, but this was my first. It was a popular class, one almost every upperclassman advised freshmen to take. So, when figuring out our schedules, Adam and I both enrolled. The subjects seemed pertinent.

During the class, the instructors took turns teaching us lessons about love, statistics about relationships, and warnings for any couples that sat in the lecture hall together. Instead of paying attention to information that might have saved our relationship, Adam and I doodled dreamily on each other's notebook.

Scrabble tonight? he wrote.

YES, I wrote.

Only six points for yes, better up your game.

ACQUIESCENCE, I replied.

After class, we walked back to our dorm building, the same one I had lived in the previous year. The biggest difference was that this year Adam was my suite-mate. As an RA, dating your residents is strictly forbidden, but considering he was still very much in the closet—even to himself—nobody was going to find out, but people speculated. One time, we came back to our hall to find *FAG* in Sharpie all over my door. I sighed, exhausted by the mountainous paperwork probably entailed in filing a report, not to mention that as an RA I'd surely be expected to call a hall meeting to discuss feelings. A moment later, Adam was appalled to find *FAG BF* scribbled all over his door. I thrilled a little that we were official now, at least according to one hateful vandal, but he was clearly humiliated.

But back to our Scrabble date—we went to our respective dorm rooms and changed into sweatpants. I set up the Scrabble board, and as Adam walked through our connecting bathroom into my room, he put on Céline Dion's greatest-hits album. He plopped onto my nine-by-nine-foot, custom-dorm-room-cut, navy carpet, leaned forward, and kissed me.

"So I've been thinking," he started.

"Oh, God."

"Shut up. Listen."

I looked into his eyes searching for signs that this wasn't anything too serious—like, he had an STD and I needed to get tested, or that we were pregnant.

"I think I might not be straight."

Sometimes, life can feel like Scrabble. You know you've got words in there somewhere, but no matter how many times you rearrange the letters, you can't seem to make sense of the jumble. Then you glance up at the person you're playing with and see him looking at you, and it's as if by simply being in your life, he's introduced you to yourself. And you look back down at your letters and everything you couldn't see before clicks into place, explained, decoded.

With exams around the corner, the main library on campus was uncomfortably packed. During finals week, the library was less of a studying opportunity than a social event. Nobody was there to study, people were there to be seen studying. With actual work to be done, Adam and I searched campus high and low for a secluded, quiet place to get work done. And by that I mean to distract each other in the privacy of our own study space. We found one in the chemistry building.

The room was cozy, but we had our own table and chalkboard, and a door for closing ourselves off from the rest of the world. Our sound track for that finals week was *Fearless* by Taylor Swift—one of the best country/pop albums of all time, which had come out a month before. The home-run single on the album was "Love Story," and we kept it on repeat, because obviously.

Maybe it was the themes in Taylor's music, maybe it was the romantic ambience of the snow falling outside our window, but we began to talk about our future together. This was one of the first times Adam had ever acknowledged that maybe, someday, he might come out to someone other than me—and that coming out might lead to being in a nonsecret relationship. And that might lead to marriage. Hearing him go on and on about his dream future of a house with a wraparound porch and a husband and kids had me reeling. Caught up in our hype, we fantasized about our kids. I got up and walked around the table, over to the chalkboard. As we debated who would take whose last name and what our kids' names would be, I wrote them out on the chalkboard to see what looked best. We were free-falling down a rabbit hole into the fantasy world of our future, and regardless of how serious *he* was, I was all-in.

We got back to studying, but I had one thing on my mind—the possibility that this guy, who I was in love with, might want to spend the rest of his life with me. Studying was hopeless. With my own love story on my mind, and Taylor's "Love Story" on a loop in my head, I spent my next study break making a lip-sync music video to Taylor's hit single, while Adam sat behind the camera trying to make me laugh. You can still find that video on my YouTube channel today, with the names of our kids erased from the chalkboard behind me (because some things are just sacred).

I texted Adam, *He's literally getting a hand job behind me.*

Adam replied, *NO THAT IS NOT HAPPENING, ASK IF THEY WANT YOU TO JOIN IN.*

I was en route north, for my second trip to Adam's hometown, this time avoiding all the speeding tickets by opting for a Greyhound bus filled with deviant strangers. The couple behind me was for sure getting intimate, and I couldn't help but laugh while texting Adam all of the alarming details. I sat there for hours, as the trip was a full day's journey, and the farther north I got, the more I could see my breath in front of me. After a full day of travel, I hopped off the bus and into the blizzard hitting Marquette, Michigan. Adam was there to meet me, bundled up from head to toe. Even though I could barely see him under all those layers, he still remained adorable.

I was visiting for New Year's, and yet again I had to play the part of Adam's college buddy.

One day we went skiing. Adam was on the ski team in high school and in the ski club in college, so he was effortlessly incredible at it. I limited myself to the slopes meant for senior citizens and toddlers, and I still struggled mightily. I was well aware of Sonny Bono's alpine demise, and I was not about to have a repeat incident.

As I slowly coasted to the bottom of a baby hill, Adam zipped by, circling me expertly. "You're really terrible at this." He chuckled.

"Listen! I never claimed to be good!"

We made our way to the ski lift, hopped on, and sat together. Unnoticed by the skiers and snowboarders below us, he held my hand in his lap. I could get used to this, and I already was. I was so accustomed to his holding my hand, but only out of sight. I was so used to his sneaking kisses, but only after looking over his shoulder. As soon as I'd start to feel resentful, I'd have to remind myself . . . this is what I signed up for. Being in a relationship with someone who is in the closet means accepting that coming out is personal. No matter what I think or how I feel, I can't rush him and I can't help anyone move quicker than he's able. So I quietly accepted that as we neared the top of the hill, he would pull his hand away from mine, and I would resume my role as his shameful secret.

Marquette, Michigan, is quaint in a lot of ways, but one of their most adorable rituals is the New Year's ball drop. In the center of town, the locals gather, layered up in long underwear, snow pants, sweaters, coats, gloves, hats, and scarves, to count down to midnight. On top of the tallest tower in town, a ball drops—exactly as in New York City's iconic Times Square tradition, except for just about everything else. Snow fell, my glasses fogged up, and as the countdown came to single digits, a crackly, old-timey rendition of "Auld Lang Syne" began to play over a public address system. Amid the sounds of noisemakers and cheers, I was overcome with emotion. Surrounded by kissing couples, I glanced over at my boyfriend, who—fearing someone might see—looked away. I'd never felt more invisible and alone.

A few days later, Adam and I took our first trip together. I had won a video-essay contest about the importance of voting, run by the Human Rights Campaign. The prize was a trip to the nation's capital. Adam and I got a ride to the airport from his aunt, who had a million questions about the situation.

"So you . . . talk about yourself on camera?" she asked.

"Yeah . . ." I trailed off. I didn't know how else to put it. I had been making videos for a little more than a year now, and it was slowly becoming a thing.

"*Thousands* of people watch him. He's *famous*," Adam joked. He knew I felt weird about it all, that it was this strange thing that many people who knew me in real life made fun of, and the last thing I wanted was people assuming I thought I was famous.

"Okay, so you won a trip . . . are you doing anything fun in DC?"

"Well, the president of the Human Rights Campaign is going to interview Tyler on his radio show," Adam bragged.

"Ohh! I want to listen. Can I listen?"

"Sure, I'll make sure Adam sends you the information," I said.

She dropped us off at the airport, and we hopped on our flight to DC. Upon arrival, we made our way to the five-star hotel they'd booked for us. "Can you believe this?" I asked, as I fell on the king-size bed. "Like, all of this . . . just because I made a YouTube video?"

"Insane." Adam fell onto the bed next to me, his face inches from mine. "Thank you for bringing me."

I smiled and reached out to cover most of his face with my hand, to shush his flattery. In retaliation, he stuck out his tongue. I laughed and groaned as I pulled away, and he rolled on top of me. In just nine months, Adam had become my best friend and the person I loved more than anything else in this world. I was Beyoncé ft. Jay Z, "Crazy in Love."

We made our way through the brisk weather to the HRC headquarters, where we met the staff of the organization. They thanked me for my video and for the work I did empowering LGBTQ+ youth, and I couldn't help but blush. I was just some silly kid in a dorm room making videos, I wasn't helping anyone. But I said thanks, and they took me to the studio where they recorded the SiriusXM radio show.

Inside the studio was the show's host and the president of the HRC, Joe Solmonese, talking into a microphone. I paced nervously, and Adam grabbed my hand. "You've got this. You're fine. If he asks you questions, don't underplay what you do. What you do is important." Adam always knew what to say. "At the end, he's gonna ask you where they can find you—they get so many listeners, so it might feel weird, but you gotta be shameless when you promote yourself."

Shameless self-promotion? Yes, I could do that.

The show's producer handed me a pair of headphones to put on, and she led me into the recording booth. She had me sit down next to Joe, who smiled at me as he finished recording a piece about marriage equality. "We're starting off January of 2009 with two states with legalized same-sex marriage. Given the progress of recent years, can you even fathom where we'll be in five years?" he said, as part of his piece.

I thought of where I'd be in five years. I couldn't have fathomed a year ago that I'd be here in Washington, DC, about to be interviewed on the radio, as if I had something important to say, or a perspective worth hearing. But maybe Adam was right? Maybe my YouTube channel did have the power to do something, to be something much bigger than myself. In five years? I hoped that in five years I'd be changing the world. Maybe I'd reach one hundred thousand subscribers. Maybe I'd write a book. Nah, stop being silly.

Joe started the interview and was kind, curious, and supportive of the unlikely path I was taking. He applauded me for being unapologetically myself, and for having the courage to tell my truth and share it with the world. Being a guest on his show was one of the most exhilarating things I had ever done, and I loved every second of it. The interview came to a close, and he glanced past me and at the people standing behind the glass outside the studio.

"And who did you bring with you today, is that your boyfriend?" Joe asked on air. Flustered, I looked back at Adam and saw terror in his eyes. Knowing this interview was live and that Adam's aunt was listening, I stumbled over my words as I denied the relationship. There I was, lying about the most important thing to me, when just a moment earlier I had been praised for speaking my truth. I felt awkward and ashamed.

The experience brought up so many questions in my head. It was one thing to feel invisible or to act like I was just his friend; these were lies of omission. But to answer a direct question from someone I respect with a blatant untruth? Was this relationship acceptable to *me*? Was this all I deserved in love? Shouldn't I want to be with someone who didn't hide being with me? Someone who would be not just unembarrassed, but even *proud* of being with me?

"It's a campus event, it literally doesn't matter," I pleaded. "There are going to be *plenty* of straight people there."

"I don't know . . . ," Adam said.

"Everyone is going. Just come. We'll have fun."

It was time for the annual MSU drag show, the momentous coming together of Michigan's top drag performers for lip syncs, shade-throwing, and glamorous shenanigans. As we entered the campus center, Adam was relieved to see the audience was far from just gays—this inclusive event had people from every background in attendance.

"Tyler?" I heard from behind me.

I spun around to find Benjamin Kirkus, a classmate from high school. We weren't that close, but we had sat next to each other in history class in high school, and he *did* let me use his employee discount to buy some boot-cut denim from Abercrombie. For as long as I'd known him, he'd seemed to be gay—but I'd never heard it out of his own mouth, so I'd let it be.

"Hey! How have you beeeeeen?" I asked, hugging him. After a little bit of catching up, I felt Adam nudge me. "Ahh, sorry, this is my friend Adam—Adam, Benjamin." I waved in Benjamin's direction. They shook hands. "Where are you sitting?"

"Up toward the front—all the seats are taken up there, but let's get together soon. Come over to my place! We can do drinks or something! You should come too," Benjamin said to Adam.

Adam and I made our way to our own seats, and the show began. Watching Adam witness his first drag show was like taking a child to Disneyland for the first time. He was wide-eyed, bewildered, and definitely in his Happiest Place on Earth. He still had great distances to go when it came to accepting his own sexuality, but he was well on his way to at least appreciating some good, wholesome, old-fashioned gay culture.

As time went on, the fun, exciting charms of a secret relationship wore thin and then threadbare. We'd argue over little things, and more of each other's habits became grating. If I was late to anything (which I often was), it was disrespect toward him. His attitude toward my online life began to shift. The more time I spent on Twitter, the more annoyed he became. I was no angel, either—I began to resent him. I was sick of hiding, pretending I didn't exist or that I wasn't a part of his life. I was so over being introduced as his "friend." I had come out years ago, and I couldn't understand why he wouldn't deal with it. You know, on my terms? I internalized his coming out as if it had something, anything, to do with me. But feelings were happening, as they do, and I felt angry, stepped on, and embarrassed.

Despite all of the things he did that upset me, I was still so infatuated with him—to a fault. I would drop anything to help him. I'd help him study. I'd shower him with gifts. Worst of all, whatever he said, went. I conceded because I thought that if I didn't, I'd lose him. So when he asked me to stop using Twitter, I completely logged out and didn't tweet for the remainder of our time together. When he asked if we could spend less weekend time visiting my family, I said okay, that was fine. I was so insecure about the stability of our relationship because nobody even knew it existed. Imagine how easy it'd be for him to drop me and never look back.

Which is exactly what he tried to do.

"We need to talk," Adam said one day, walking into my room.

"Oooookayyyyyy?" I replied, feeling it coming.

"I don't think we should be together anymore."

My heart sank, and my stomach dropped, and I didn't know

what to do. This man was the first person I ever loved, the first person I ever saw a future with, the only man I could imagine myself raising kids with. Sure we fought, and sure we got under each other's skin, but in my head you don't tell someone you love them or come up with baby names with them if you can't handle working through your issues.

"I think we should be seeing other people."

I looked at him in the eyes. *Who are you? Who else do you want to see? What am I not giving you? What else is there that I haven't done for you?*

Just when I thought he couldn't say anything worse, he did.

"I still want to be friends." He grabbed my knee. The same knee he used to hold while he would drive us around town. How could someone whose comforting grasp sent chills down my spine somehow become a vague acquaintance that I'd meet for coffee every once in a while? How could I go from loving someone so intensely to simply waving in his direction if I saw him in the cafeteria? I was devastated and confused.

I said nothing, and he got up and went to his own room. After a few minutes, I heard his front door open and close. I rushed to my own front door and looked through the peephole. He walked down the hall. Pressing my body against the door, I watched until he was gone. My eye strained to catch one last glimpse of him, but he had vanished. My eyes welled. I walked slowly back to my couch, sat down, and began to cry quietly. I had invested so much of myself into this relationship, and the prospect of its disappearing made me feel violently ill.

I got out my phone and dialed the only person I knew had been through something like this—my mom. She'd faced divorce, she knew what this felt like, and she'd made it through. *She'll know what to say and do.* As soon as she answered, I burst. My quiet tears swelled into violent sobs as I tried to make sense of the situation. No matter what she said, nothing could stop me from the hysteria I was spiraling into, but one phrase she kept repeating stuck in my mind: "You will get through this."

Hours later, I heard his door open and shut and could hear him stirring next door. I walked through our conjoined bathroom and knocked on his door.

"Come in."

Before turning the handle, I glanced at the bathroom mirror. My face was red, my eyes were puffy, and the top of my T-shirt was damp from tears. I was a mess, and I had clearly been a mess for the hours he had been gone. *Maybe now he'll see how much he means to me,* I thought, fully aware of how disordered that sounded.

I walked into his room. He was sitting on the edge of the bed, sanding down a table he was refurbishing. He loved to take old furniture and make it shine like new. He looked up at me, and when he saw the condition I was in, his face broke. He set down the sandpaper, stood up, and hugged me, long and tight.

"We can't break up," I whispered into his shoulder. "I love you."

Adam pulled back and sat back down on the bed. "I just feel like I have no idea what's out there. If I'm supposed to be with you, shouldn't I have something else to compare this relationship to? You've dated plenty of guys. You're the only guy I've ever even kissed."

He made sense. And maybe he was right. Even though I couldn't even imagine him with another guy, and the mere thought of it was repulsive, the only idea even more repulsive was that of losing him. In a heartbeat, I made a decision. It was a compromise, a suggestion I would forever wish I could take back.

"Why don't we try being in an open relationship?" At least I could maybe be the man he came home to afterward. Maybe I could be the guy he raised kids with, and if he needed to get off elsewhere, he could go, take care of it, and be home in time for dinner. I was ready to sacrifice part of my fantasy life, in exchange for the only guy with whom I thought I could reach that fantasy life.

"You'd let me see other guys?"

I looked him in the eye, long and hard. *I guess we're doing this.*

Being your own boyfriend's wingman can create some awkward moments. For example, seeing your boyfriend shave in the bathroom you share, much like the way he'd shave before a date with you, might lead you to *want* to ask what he's up to tonight, but you already know. Sometimes I'd be sitting on his bed, and he'd ask which of two date ideas sounded better. I didn't know if he meant for me or for another guy. Usually, he meant another guy.

I acted peachy keen, as if this were the *exact* conversation I wanted to be having. I acted as if I were so happy he was dating, and if he needed a ride, just call me! Part of me was morbid enough to want to know every detail, because if he told me everything, at least nothing could be a devastatingly shocking surprise down the line. So I let him tell me these things, and I let him ask me for advice, and I let him continue to date. If he was doing it in front of my eyes, at least we were being truthful with each other—and if we couldn't quite do monogamy, at least we could try honesty. Or so I told myself.

Spring break that year was spent like one long double date, with Adam and me and our friend Korey and his boyfriend, Patrick. The four of us had gotten close over the past few months, and we had decided to spend spring break on vacation in Cancún. Subsequent to our new arrangement, it was to be the longest time that I had Adam all to myself. I couldn't have been happier.

We opted for an all-inclusive resort, which was split into two pool areas: one for youthful, beer-guzzling spring breakers, the other for old ladies wearing fanny packs and visors. Obviously, we hung out with the grandmas.

The most hilarious moment of that trip happened when the four of us were lounging poolside, a margarita in one hand and a guacamole-laden chip in the other. Our side of the resort was quiet, and every chair was occupied by someone over seventy. Out of the blue, a bloodcurdling scream echoed across the pool. All eyes zeroed in on an old woman who sat bolt upright, horrified, holding a pickle.

"That sky-rat dropped a pickle on me!" she proclaimed, answering the stares all around her. Apparently, a seagull had swooped down, snatched up a pickle from someone's plate, then air-dropped it on the woman's bare midriff. I like to be-

lieve the bird was slut-shaming her for wearing a two-piece as a septuagenarian. Obviously, her exclamation became *the* iconic quote for the entire trip.

At night, we'd continue drinking and make our way to the dance floor, where Adam would drunkenly flail as if nobody were watching. Korey's boyfriend, Patrick, would be so embarrassed by it that he would quietly pray that literally nobody was watching. One night we got especially drunk, and Adam and I regressed to arguing about one thing and another, and we angrily fought all the way back to our suite. It was one of those drunken arguments that last so long that you start to sober up halfway through and completely forget what you've been arguing about for all those hours. We were fighting to fight and airing long-suppressed grievances haphazardly.

After hours of screams, tears, and accusations, the sun began to rise outside our window. I lay there, still. This was not the spring break I had imagined. This was not the relationship I had dreamed of.

Adam sat up. "Do you love me?"

"Are you an idiot?"

"I love you, but I'm still trying to figure everything out. I'm sorry, but you were the one who said it was okay that I dated other people."

He was right. I couldn't blame him for his behavior if his behavior was exactly what I suggested. But I did because, why couldn't he read my mind?

"Do you know I love you?"

I sat there in bed and thought about his question. *Did* I know that? So much of our relationship was spent with him in the closet that the majority of our time together was with him acting like he *didn't* love me. Maybe I had started to believe it. My infatuation with him and lack of respect for myself allowed him to do whatever he wanted. And there I was, still not getting what I wanted, even after all those compromises. I shrugged my shoulders, looked at him, and said, exhausted, "I don't know."

He took my hand and led me to our suite's balcony. He attached his earbuds to his iPod and scrolled through his music library. Pushing play, he slipped the iPod into the elastic of his underwear, placed one earbud in one of my ears, and one earbud in one of his, and pulled me into his arms. There, we began to slow-dance, in our underwear, as the music began to play.

Joshua Radin's "The Fear You Won't Fall" said it all, once again. We swayed in each other's arms as the sun rose over the water, and he rested his head on my shoulder. I began to cry, not out of happiness or sadness, but because I had no idea how I felt, or what was happening. Nothing was clear with Adam, and I had no clue what was going to happen when we returned to Michigan.

The last couple months of our relationship were rough. Fights got intense, and time spent together became awkward and uncomfortable. It was as if we were learning how to not know each other. A week before our breakup, we went to New York City for a getaway weekend. We got dinner at this little hole-in-the-wall. We sat in silence, chewing our food, and it was worse than dinner with a stranger. I tried to keep the conversation going, but he didn't have much left to say. Even to the pitiful end, I held on to the chance that we could somehow work through it.

Even until our very last day together, I felt deep, foolish, hopeful love.

One lesson I learned from my relationship with Adam is that being dumped is especially hard. While the other person immediately seems fine, you feel like it's the end of your life. More than your pain, it's this vile contrast that is so insupportable. Being dumped by Adam (twice) and how seemingly unruffled he was about it (twice!) made me realize that his relationship with me ended long before mine with him. He got a head start on his grieving, without anyone informing me that I should start mine too. His negative behavior leading up to the breakup was not just him acting out. It was him dealing with the relationship's end.

Now I think of breaking up as moving. Imagine you have your own house, full of your own boxes. A person you meet has his own house, full of his own boxes. When you have a relationship with that person, you shack up in a third house, into which you can each put any number of your boxes. You shouldn't move them all in at once, or else you will seem too eager. And don't dawdle too much either, or you will seem skittish about commitment. You kind of aim to match each other's pace, so that the power balance feels fair and equal. Happy marriage—at least ideally—would be the situation in which both parties enthusiastically choose to keep all of their boxes in their shared house. Conversely, when someone starts to doubt the relationship, he might move a box or two back into his own house, just in case. While he's weighing his options, he may transport a few more boxes to the safety of his own home. When he's ready to take back his final few boxes, he breaks up with you. If you were too infatuated to see it coming, there you are, with all of your boxes in the shared house, and none in the security of your own home.

We may have been in an open relationship, but I think he knew I couldn't handle the truth of the situation. Lord knows I never pursued anyone else. I was just turning a blind eye and waiting patiently for the best. Adam broke up with me in May, but he'd quietly been moving his boxes out for months.

Before we broke up, Adam asked me if I'd be interested in a threesome with Benjamin, the high school friend I had introduced him to at the drag show. Confused, I said no. As soon as we were officially split, the two of them became inseparable. I guess I had found where he had been moving his boxes. They were together for years following that.

Dealing with our breakup was the worst pain I'd ever felt in my life. I turned cynical and angry. I focused more energy on wishing the worst for certain people than wishing the best for myself. I'd lock myself in my room for days. Like a demented prisoner, I'd rush to the peephole of my door anytime I heard anyone walking by. I'd obsessively stalk Adam's social media profiles and investigate anyone who ever interacted with him online. I tried to date, but I felt as if nobody measured up. And to what? This asshole—the one that got away.

This was the only time I ever seriously considered suicide. It was the only time I've ever called the Trevor Project, a suicide and crisis prevention lifeline, available to chat if you're in need of help. I was in a terrible place, sobbing all day, every day, dreading waking up, and disliking being alive. When the Trevor Project volunteer answered my call and asked what was wrong, I felt silly explaining my issues. Just saying them out loud to a stranger felt like I was figuring them out myself. The parts that were blurriest in my mind became clearer, more focused—newly visible—with the help of the kind person on the other end.

I may have only called the Trevor Project once, but that was enough to pull me out from the dark hole I had dug. I wouldn't have been able to escape had I not reached out for help. I later interned for the Trevor Project, and I've dedicated my platform online to raising money and awareness for them ever since. I'm so grateful.

To move on, I read self-help books such as *It's Called a Breakup Because It's Broken* and *He's Just Not That into You*. I went to therapy. Being able to see that I wasn't alone, and that my heartbreak was not necessarily unique, helped me see that others had gotten through it. I decided that I had cried enough, and I had complained enough, and my friends were sick of hearing my sad song on repeat. The true remedy for heartbreak was time. Where I once hung a calendar counting down the days until I could see Adam, I now put up a calendar counting how many days I could go without sulking. It was a don't-break-the-chain encouragement technique. Every day I crossed off was a day that I actively decided to take care of *me*. I hung it over my peephole, and anytime I was tempted to see if it was Adam walking by my room with another guy, I was visually reminded that I was on a journey of improving myself, not wallowing in the past. The best way out is always through.

Nowadays, more than five years later, Adam and I are good friends. We've forgiven each other and ourselves for the ways we disrespected or manipulated each other. We've since supported each other through breakups, career challenges, family changes, and more. He's seen me at my highest, my lowest, and everywhere in between. Although it took years for me to understand him and learn from my time with him, I'm happy to say that I do think I have learned. Most recently, he attended the Chicago stop of my Slumber Party Tour, and he got to see the craziness of the community we've created, dear readers, together.

We also got together recently for a dinner in New York City, at a hole-in-the-wall restaurant similar to the one in which we'd eaten in silence so long ago. It was five years later, and this time we had plenty to talk about. We reminisced about all the good times we had and how much we had been through together. We had been in a relationship for only a year, but we came to realize just how profound the impacts we had on each other were. He asked me if I believed in the concept of a "love of your life" or a "one that got away" or a "soul mate."

"Yes, one hundred percent, for sure, without a doubt do I believe in a 'love of your life.' But I think that we have multiple loves of our lives, who are supposed to join us at just the right times. Throughout our entire time on earth, we end up meeting all of them."

Adam was such an important love of my life. To look back on our relationship as anything other than so many moments to learn from would be a disservice to ourselves. It would be a missed opportunity to grow and prepare for the *next* love of my life (if it's you, *well, hello!*). Every relationship ends, unless one doesn't. Everything we've learned from the relationships leading up to that last one has been the training we needed to make this final one last.

"And as far as a 'one that got away'? Do I believe in that?" I smiled. "Well, yes. I definitely consider myself to be *your* one that got away."

unnecessary
holiday traditions

SOME AMERICAN HOLIDAY TRADITIONS ARE SO unnecessary.

·•●•·

Don't fucking pinch me on St. Patrick's Day because I'm not wearing green. That is assault, and green is not slimming, and I need you to respect that.

·•●•·

I'm twenty-six and still don't have a clue how the groundhog situation works. If on a day in February, a groundhog comes out of his hole and sees his shadow, he somehow predicts the weather for the next *month or two*, which not even Doppler radar can do. Is this is some next-level witchcraft? Not to mention, as someone who aspires to someday work as a local weather forecaster, I feel threatened by this lazy rodent and his dubious prediction skills.

•• • ••

Please don't sing "Happy Birthday" to me. Not only are you violating the copyright of the original composer, but it's also the most insufferable fifteen seconds you could inflict on me. Why do we further punish people for aging, which is already punishment enough?

•• • ••

Columbus Day celebrates a man who started a mass genocide. Somehow, kids get this day off to celebrate, yet they don't get off the day Beyoncé dropped her album? America, figure out your shit.

•• • ••

April Fools' is the worst of all holidays. Nobody of quality wants to participate; we just have to be aware of it and paranoid that someone shitty is going to do something annoying or horrible. The only people who are into this are fuckboys who abuse it.

The worst part of April Fools' Day is that some of the terrible things that happen to you turn out not to be tricks. Once, I was supposed to fly to a speaking engagement, and I fell asleep at the gate during a layover in a North Carolina airport. When I woke up, the gate was empty, and I was sure it was an elaborate April Fools' prank. Unfortunately, less elaborately, I had simply missed my flight.

Part of me wonders if the true joke of April Fools' is that every year it's already April and I've yet to figure out what's going on.

•• • ••

Black History Month is a struggle because we have to put up with dumb white people asking why we don't have a White History Month (spoiler: every month is your month due to the white privilege you refuse to acknowledge; literally shut up).

• • • •

I have no problems with 7/11, also known as Free Slurpee Day. It is proof that God loves us and wants us to be happy.

• • • •

February 29 needs to be discussed. Every four years, we have an extra day in our calendar and call it a leap day, and everyone just kind of goes along with it. But why don't we do something radical on that day to celebrate? Like something completely outrageous. I've got ideas. Hear me out. What if, on February 29, we . . .

• Give women equal pay.

• Don't shoot people based on racial bias.

• Gays and straights alike accept the existence of bisexuals.

• People stop accusing me of having a hook head.

Let me know what y'all think! Maybe if everyone likes these the first year, we can just make them an everyday thing?

• • • •

Halloween is perfect. Please enjoy me in a wizard costume.

crash course

IF THERE'S ONE PIECE OF ADVICE I CAN GIVE YOU in this book, it's the following: don't, under any circumstances, ride in a car with me driving.

I aggressively run into things, back up into things, have no depth perception, often forget which buttons and knobs do what, and am easily distracted. But enough about my sex life! Back to my driving skills! When it comes to driving, I'm what an expert might call . . . "the worst."

When I turned sixteen, I had taken driver's education and was ready to test my skills in my first official driver's test. I had been practicing for months, and although I had extreme anxiety on highways, cul-de-sacs, main roads, back roads, freeways, driveways, and parking lots, I was vaguely able to get from point A to point B. I'd just have to hope that nobody and nothing was even remotely in my way, ever. Thankfully, when I took my test, I wasn't that terrible! The only fail-worthy error that I made—not stopping at a stop sign in a parking lot—happened while the examiner was looking over his shoulder, talking to my stepdad in the backseat. Thank *God*.

With my license in hand, I was ready to take the road by storm. Unfortunately, I kind of did that literally. Before I had saved up enough money to buy my own car, I was allowed to use my older sister's car to drive to school and work. I was working at Arby's, and one day I had a shift immediately after school. As soon as the bell rang after sixth period, I rushed into the bathroom to change into my grease-stained Arby's uniform, and I promptly made my way to my sister's car.

I tapped my thumbs on the steering wheel along to the beat of Lifehouse's "You and Me," while glancing up and down from the traffic to the clock. With traffic this tight, I was never going to make it in time. As the chorus rang in, I began to sing along, while inching forward impatiently. At a traffic light, thinking I had a chance to make my left turn before the light changed to red, I went for it. At the same time, an oncoming SUV decided to attempt it also. As the humongous vehicle charged toward me, full speed, my singing voice involuntarily crescendoed. As I slammed on the brakes, my body whipped forward aggressively as my sister's little Oldsmobile collided with the SUV, coming to a complete stop in the middle of the crowded intersection. The wind was knocked out of me, and I slowly opened my eyes and looked up. Lifehouse continued to play on the radio with eerily accurate lyrics: "What day is it? And in what month? This clock never seemed so alive."

Well, now I'm officially going to be late.

My body was fine, but my spirit was shattered. I stepped out of the car in full Arby's garb, as the population of my entire high school inched around the collision to get a better view. The driver of the SUV hopped down from her car and stomped over to yell at me, but I paid her no attention. With her screams in the background, I stood next to what looked like a Mothers Against Drunk Driving demonstration. As my classmates drove by, I made eye contact with all of them, one by one. Me, my totaled car, and my grease-stained Arby's uniform were on full display.

Just when I thought my lowest point had been reached, my high school crush, Nick, pulled toward the collision. As I realized it was him approaching, my heart leaped into my throat. Lifehouse continued to play as he drove by, seemingly in slow motion. A single tear of shame rolled down my cheek, but it was effortlessly repelled by my polyester Arby's uniform. Maybe it was this shameful event that led Nick to go along with my yearbook picture imposition years later.

Soon after, a cop showed up to file a police report, but when she saw the damage done to my dignity, she let me go without writing me a ticket. The car was towed away. I walked home to use the landline to call work and explain the situation, as well as to deliver the bad news to my sister about her car. Not my best moment.

After that car was totaled, it was back to being dropped off at work by my parents. This made getting shifts increasingly difficult, which made saving up money even more impossible. When I was finally able to afford my own car, I talked to my parents about the options listed in the local newspaper. Although almost everything was out of my price range, one car in particular stood out, and not just because of the low price. Its appearance was a bit uncanny, but beggars can't be choosers. We made plans to go see it that Sunday morning.

In the meantime, my friends and I were planning to head an hour southeast to the neighboring college town of Ann Arbor for a Saturday night out. A few of our friends who were now freshmen in college invited us to come visit, and we'd been counting down for the several weeks leading up to our excursion. Although I had plans to check out the car the very next morning, nothing was getting between me and our night of scheduled debauchery.

We made our way down to Ann Arbor and arrived in time for pregaming in our friends' small dorm room. Back then, budgets were tight, alcohol was bottom shelf, and our bodies were far from ready for the abuse we were about to inflict on them. After a night of way too much cheap cherry vodka, I awoke to my flip phone's alarm, and my eyes shot open. What. Happened. Last. Night? I looked at the clock and bolted upright as soon as I realized what time it was. I shook my groaning friends out of their slumber and struggled to get everyone shuffled back into the car for the ride home. I was in such a frenzied hustle that I barely realized how hungover I was myself—that is, until we started the car and pulled out of the driveway.

While my friend drove us back toward our hometown, I attempted to focus on not dying. Window completely down while driving seventy on the highway, face covered with a coat, head angled just so to minimize the spinning . . . I was a hot mess. Maybe this is why teenagers aren't allowed to drink in America. I managed to hold down the remaining vodka in my stomach as it nostalgically tried to revisit my mouth that morning. Suddenly, I felt the car come to a full stop. I removed the coat from my head and saw my home. As I climbed out of the backseat, my mom emerged from the front door.

"Well, look who it is!" she declared, as I trudged up the driveway, stifling my groans of agony. "Just in time to help clean up dog poop in the backyard!" My parents knew when I was suffering from a night too fun and a morning too rough, and they found pleasure in subsequently pushing me to the edge. "I can literally smell the vodka on you from here," my mom said, side-eyeing me as she handed me a shovel. I made my way painfully into the backyard. "Hurry up, we've got to go look at that car as soon as you're done."

Our dogs loved to shit. It was their medium of self-expression, and during the summer months, their art took on new levels of sensory complexity. We had a garbage can that we piled their poop into, and in the heat of the sun it was probably the least pleasant experience this side of ever. Imagine a shit casserole, cooked overnight on low in the Crock-Pot of a giant. Now imagine that experience combined with the worst hangover of your life, and you've got yourself the perfect storm to induce projectile vomiting all over your backyard. Which is exactly what happened.

My mom clapped and cheered as I sprayed down the lawn, and she cackled as she closed the sliding glass door. What a peach. I picked up the last of the dog poop and made my way inside to attempt to shower and then go check out that damn car.

My second drive of the day was far better than the first, but still a struggle. Take all of the elements of the first, and add a lecture from my stepdad (a substance-abuse therapist). I held my vomit behind gritted teeth, and we finally made it to the seller's house. And there was the car, in the driveway, exactly as advertised.

It was in my price range for a reason. That reason stuck out like a big, red sore thumb. The car, a blue Oldsmobile, looked to be in pretty good condition, but when you circled to its other side, you saw the extent of its . . . character. The driver's side front door was bright red, making it perhaps the most patriotic car in the city. I began to feel myself getting woozy again.

I continued to inspect the car as my stepdad made his way to the front door of the house and rang the doorbell. Out stepped a little old woman, who stayed up on the porch talking to my stepdad. They chatted a bit, and he pointed over his shoulder back at my mom and me. We waved and made our way up to the porch.

"That car has pizzazz!" the lady yelled, as if we all were hard of hearing. My head throbbed. "Let me go find the paper-work inside."

I made my way down the steps and felt my damp forehead. Oh, no. Nauseated, I looked back at my mom. She gave me a look that said, *I swear to God, Mathew Tyler Oakley, if you even dare . . .* I replied with a look that said, *Forgive me, Mother, for I am about to sin.* I covered my mouth and scooted fast—past the red-doored, blue car, through the old woman's bushes, and around the side of the house. When I couldn't step any far-ther and my mouth couldn't hold any more, my hand flung in a wide arc and my mouth opened and out came the rest of the shots from the night before. The splashing sound was disgusting enough to keep the vomit coming. Hands on my knees, I heaved until I was empty.

Wiping my mouth with the back of my hand, I slowly straightened up to standing, only to meet a pair of eyes in the window I had puked under. There, through the window screen, was the little old woman, paperwork in hand.

Needless to say, I didn't attempt to haggle on the price. Instead, I drove home with a brand-new used, multicolored car, and a heart full of shame.

Over time, I came to love that car. Fifty percent of the time, it was the easiest car to spot in any parking lot. That car served me well for the year I had it, until I totaled it in another car accident.

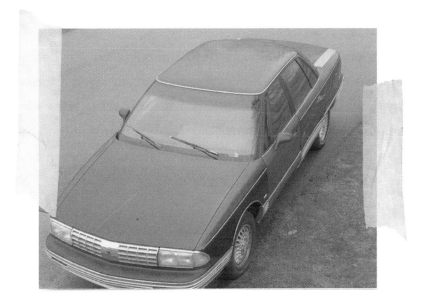

From there, I bought my brother's Jeep from him, which was way too big for me to handle, and it was way too bouncy for me to ever feel like I was in control. Once, while driving it, I was making my way around a corner during a thunderstorm, when all of a sudden I gasped from the thumps of running over something. I kept driving for a moment, replaying in my mind what I thought I'd seen, before I pulled over. No. There's no way. I picked up my phone and called my mom.

"Hello?"

"I think I ran over a baby."

"You what?!"

I explained what had happened, and she started screaming that if this was a prank, I would lose my two hours of Internet for that day. I assured her that I was, in fact, most likely a murderer, and that it wasn't my fault, because who puts their baby in the street during a thunderstorm?

"Get out of the car, and go find that baby and make sure that it was *not a baby*."

I stepped into the pouring rain and made my way back to the scene of the crime. I was going to be *so* annoyed if today I turned out to be a baby murderer, but I was going to be even *more* annoyed if today I found no dead baby in the road and got soaked for no reason. Thankfully, what I thought was a dead baby ended up being a plastic grocery bag full of leaves, and I was not a murderer. Yet.

Fast-forward a few months, and I totaled that car, too. It happened at just the right time, though. I was about to become a college freshman, and my first year on campus I wasn't allowed to have a parking pass. Everything happens for a reason or something.

My sophomore year, when I was allowed a parking pass, I

decided to go car shopping once again, but this time at a real used-car dealership. I missed my flashy red-doored blue car and wanted something that said *Hello!* just as much as it said *I know you can see me and you should probably stay out of my way*. When I saw what was going to be my next car, it was love at first sight.

If you listen to my podcast *Psychobabble* or watch my videos, you may know that I have a habit of naming colors. A color is never just gray . . . it's more likely to be ashes-of-my-enemies gray, or maybe underbelly-of-a-happy-whale gray . . . but never just gray. This habit may have started when I bought my next car—a subtly ripe kiwi-green Ford Focus. It was visually loud, and I was obsessed. This car took a little longer for me to total, but when I did, it was my worst crash yet.

It was Christmas Eve, and I was home for the holiday. With nobody showing up anywhere close to me on Grindr (a gay dating app which I'll tell you a horror story about later in the book), I decided to take matters into my own hands. As I was en route to Chicago to meet up with a boy I met online (sorry, Mom), blasting the *Disney Princess: The Ultimate Song Collection* CD, I hit a spot of black ice and went spiraling out of control. I didn't hit any other cars, but running into the dividers on the highway was enough to squash my Ford Focus like a subtly ripe kiwi.

Stuck with my car facing backward on the highway divider, I arranged for a tow to the closest mechanic in Indiana, halfway between Michigan and Illinois. With dents on all sides of my car and my hood bent and unclosable, the mechanics strongly advised me not to finish the trip, as it was likely that something would go very wrong. Blinded by the prospect of literally getting dick for Christmas, I forged on. Neither snow nor rain nor gloom of night was going to stand between me and a hookup.

With my hood held down by several bungee cords, I made my way to Chicago, clunked my wreck into a parking spot, and enjoyed Christmas and New Year's exactly how I imagined I would. After that, I carefully made my way back home to Michigan for the rest of my winter break. Unfortunately, my thirst for hooking up got the better of me yet again, and after a brief Facebook conversation with an ex living on the other side of Michigan, I was lured into another booty-call road trip before school started back up. I was insatiable.

With so little time between my last hookup excursion and my next, I hadn't yet gotten my car looked at properly by a mechanic. Grave mistake. I hit the road with the janky repairs made by the Indiana mechanic. I felt sure this was a safe way to travel.

In the dead of night, I was halfway across Michigan, singing along to Adele's *19* album, preparing for a weekend of rekindled romance. Perhaps I hit the high note too well, because one of the bungee cords snapped. The rest of my cords began to snap, one by one, flinging into the darkness of the night. In a single moment, all were gone, and with a crash, my car's hood flung up, smashing into my windshield, cracks spiderwebbing across the glass, and totally obstructing my view of the road. My singing pitch suddenly veered sharp.

I was driving full speed down the highway, blind. Adele's lyrics seemed to address my situation: *Should I give up? Or should I just keep chasin' pavements?*

Timely question, Adele. Or perhaps I should make like

Carrie Underwood and let Jesus take the wheel? But, no, I couldn't trust anyone else to handle this kiwi beauty, not even the son of God. I put on my hazard lights, slowed down, and cautiously moved over to the right lane until I reached the road's edge. Then I drove five miles per hour to the next exit, scooted into the closest gas station, and got my car repaired properly. No, I'm just messing with you. I bought more bungee cords and made my way to my hookup's house via slower, more manageable back roads.

It was another fun weekend, but I'd say the most awkward part was having to ask his dad for car help. For some conservative dads, having a gay son can be challenging, but having to help your gay son's booty call fix his car? This hookup was no strings attached, but had bungee cords galore. Oh, well, at least I got laid.

I drove home after that weekend, and my car was beat every which way, with dents, scrapes, cracks in the windshield, and a busted hood tied down haphazardly. My car literally couldn't look worse—or so I thought. My low-fuel light came on midtrip, though I barely noticed due to the constellation of flashing alerts on my dashboard. It was like a Christmas display in Crackville.

I pulled off the highway at the next exit and turned into the nearest gas station. Unfortunately, my lack of depth perception got the best of me once again. After what I had endured that week, I couldn't help but cackle as realized I was I scraping the entire side of my car against the bright yellow pole next to the gas pump. Strangers pumping gas watched with a look of terror, eyeing me as I laughed hysterically at my pump. I filled the car with just enough fuel to make it home, and not a drop more—Lord knows I'd never be driving this hunk of junk ever again.

Near the end of my college career, I came dangerously close to totaling my mom's car. I had borrowed it to drive to a job interview at Google. During my drive, I spent the entire trip overthinking everything from my résumé to my memorized interview answers—so I decided to take my mind off my qualifications and focus on reasons why I would totally get the job. First, I looked adorable. As I flipped my visor down to look at my flawless hair in the mirror, out of nowhere a huge black spider fell onto my lap. Swatting every which way and yelping like a terrified schoolgirl, I swerved all over the road and across multiple lanes of traffic. I arrived safely, but my anxiety had been ratcheted to a new peak, which was not helpful in a job interview. I did not get that job, which I entirely blame on my mom. Who hides a live spider in her visor to purposely terrify her son? Monsters, that's who.

Since graduating college and moving to Los Angeles, I've had only one accident, a fender bender. It happened while I was parking at the house of my good friend and fellow YouTuber-turned-cultural-icon Grace Helbig. Grace is a multi-talented media mogul, with her own book (*Grace's Guide*, pick up a copy!) and TV show on E!, but back then, she was just a YouTuber who I thought was brilliant. We were getting together to film for the first time in person, and I was so nervous. She's always seemed effortlessly hilarious, and I've always felt try-hard and unfunny in comparison. Having spent way too long getting lost in the Hollywood Hills trying to find her house, I was mortified when I parked and scraped the entire side of her car with mine. She laughed until she cried, then made me a cocktail. We toasted to the beautiful start of our new friendship and got so drunk that I had to spend the night. Bless her soul.

Nowadays, I opt to spend less time behind the wheel and more time in the passenger seat. Most of that experience is spent gasping at oncoming traffic, recoiling anytime I think we're about to get in an accident, and slamming my foot into my invisible driver's-education passenger-brake pedal. So I guess I have a second piece of advice to offer: don't ride in a car with me while *you're* driving, either.

a love lesson

ACH TIME HE KICKED ME, I SCREAMED. I cowered on the floor of Justin's apartment, praying that his roommates would walk through the front door. Even if they were as blackout drunk as he was, or high out of their minds, or tripping on acid, they would know this was wrong, and they would stop him. I cried and groaned and pleaded between each blow, until he exhausted his rage and stomped off to his room. He locked his bedroom door, and I crawled over to his living-room couch, laid myself on it, and sobbed into the cushion, wondering how I'd hide my bruises the next day. *Why did I choose him?*

When I first went on a date with Justin, I was still mourning my failed relationship with Adam, and I felt lonelier than ever before. I missed having a blanket, but Justin was woven from barbed wire. I tried to make do with a blanket that offered not warmth and comfort, but puncture wounds and tetanus.

Even after the night he beat me, I decided to give him another chance. I stayed with him because, in my head, his behavior felt like what I had chosen for myself. He didn't seem like someone who would beat up his boyfriend. He *did* seem like someone who could possibly drink too much, and everyone knows what can happen when you drink too much, right? These are the doomed spirals of logic your mind will descend when you think being alone means being lonely, and that being lonely is worse than being mistreated.

Throughout my writing of this book, I wondered if I'd write about my experience with physical abuse. One of the biggest reasons I used to talk myself out of ever mentioning it publicly was that it only happened once. And who knew what my friends and family might think of me for having stayed with him after it happened?

The one thing that outweighed all my doubts was the consideration of you, dear reader. I wish I had read a book that told me what I shouldn't be doing, as I was doing it. While I can't tell you how to live your life, I can certainly suggest that you deserve love, and that love doesn't abuse you.

I never knew that love didn't hurt. My childhood was spent navigating divorces and custody battles, and in my head, love was war. You fought and you made up, and those highs and lows were called passion. But I'm opting out of that mentality. Sure, relationships include arguments, but pain is not a side effect of love. Sometimes frustration or confusion, okay, but I don't think *pain* is going to be a part of my love ever again. If someone is harming you physically, mentally, emotionally, or sexually, that is not love.

I'm young, and I don't have all the answers. I'll probably make a ton of mistakes before I figure it out. But *none* of them will involve tolerating abuse in the name of love.

beyoncé for the day

1. GO DOOR-TO-DOOR—It's incredibly important for me to use this day to freak people the fuck out, and there's no better way to surprise people than to show up and ring their doorbell. When they open the door, I'd simply say in a sultry voice, "Yes, I'm Beyoncé."

2. PRETEND AN ALBUM IS COMING—When Beyoncé was recording her secret album, *Beyoncé*, she shot some footage for the video in public. To keep her new music a mystery, she had headphones in her ears and walked around lip-synching to a camera. Now that people know this, I'd walk around everywhere with earbuds in and a cameraman. Keep those other, basic pop divas on their toes.

3. SING INTO A MIRROR—Beyoncé is obviously one of the greatest vocalists in the world. Although being Tyler Oakley does have its perks (I once was a guest on *The Ellen DeGeneres Show* and Cher follows me on Twitter), being Tyler Oakley won't get me front-row tickets to a Beyoncé concert. Thus, I would sing into a mirror to give myself the best seat in the house for a mini-acoustic set.

4. OVERTHROW THE PATRIARCHY—Duh.

5. SING THE NATIONAL ANTHEM TO THE LOCALS—Beyoncé has already snatched wigs at the inauguration of the president of the United States by slaying the national anthem, but if I were her, I'd take it local. Bust into some small-town football game, swipe the microphone from a local high school choirgirl, push her down into a puddle while I'm at it, and go out onto the field to deliver some patriotic vocal fireworks. I'd then drop the mic and make eye contact with exactly nobody as I exited through the stands.

6. SIGN DOLLAR BILLS—Not everyone can get a Beyoncé autograph, so I'd sign a stack of dollar bills and go on a shopping spree at a dollar store. Put those Washingtons into rotation for the common folk. Y'all are welcome.

7. CALL UP LATAVIA, LETOYA, AND FARRAH—Everyone gives Michelle and Kelly grief for playing second fiddle to Beyoncé, but can you imagine being LaTavia Roberson, LeToya Luckett, or Farrah Franklin? They were all also once in Destiny's Child, and nobody remembers them. I'd call them up and give 'em some motivational pep talks. Lord knows they need 'em.

8. CALL UP APPLE—No, not Gwyneth Paltrow's daughter. The world needs a Beyoncé emoji, and if Beyoncé asked for it, Apple understands it would have to deliver.

9. SASS PEOPLE ON TWITTER—As Beyoncé, I'd be interested in searching my indirects on Twitter (that's when people tweet about you but don't tag you, assuming you won't find it) and sassing out people who talk shit about me. Obviously, I'd be very busy that day.

10. TEATIME WITH THE GIRLS—I can't be all go, go, go, all day long. I'm going to need to recharge. Oprah, Ellen, Gaga, Michelle Obama, Cher, Caitlyn Jenner . . . everyone's coming to tea.

11. BREAK RECORDS WITH BLUE IVY—If you're the child of Beyoncé, you've got big shoes to fill, so I'd start Blue Ivy's life out on the right foot. Help her break some Guinness records before she starts preschool. I mean, even when she was two days old, she already broke a record by becoming the youngest person to ever debut in the *Billboard* charts. Why not break some more records?

12. POLISH MY GRAMMYS—There is nothing more satisfying than cleaning my Grammys. Obviously, I would then snapchat pictures of them to all my less talented vocalist friends. Not naming names, but just try comparing my mountain of gold to your MTV Latin America Award for Best Ringtone in 2009.

13. DROP AN ALBUM—No, not in the way you think. Nobody can do that in a day. Well, okay, maybe Beyoncé could. But, no, I'd go to Best Buy, pick up a CD, clumsily let it fall to the floor, and then make a joke about pulling a Beyoncé.

14. SELF-PROMO—I'd carry over some Tyler Oakley tendencies while being Beyoncé, and one of them would have to be shameless self-promotion. I'd be tweeting out my iTunes links, pushing the LIKE button on my Vevo videos, everything. If you've got a platform, promote, girl! By the way, follow me on Twitter: @tyleroakley.

15. ENTER A DRAG COMPETITION—Drag queens love to perform Beyoncé songs. They're strong, powerful, loud, and dramatic. If I were Beyoncé, I'd go to a gay bar on a Friday night and compete as a Beyoncé-impersonating drag queen. Some queens are so good, I'd probably come in second.

16. PROMOTE *ARTPOP*—Lady Gaga needs all the help she can get right now.

17. RE-CREATE "LADY MARMALADE"—In 2001, Christina Aguilera, Lil' Kim, Mýa, Pink, and Missy Elliott joined forces to put out "Lady Marmalade," an all-girls single that slayed the charts, as well as my heart. A decade later, we *need* an updated version. If I were Beyoncé, I'd use my vocal powers and my impressive list of contacts to unite the voices needed to outslay the previous version. Gaga, Carrie, Nicki, Robyn, check your texts. I need you.

18. GO TO STARBUCKS IN A MASK—I'd order my usual grande iced coffee with soy, and when they asked for my name to write it on my cup, I'd dramatically scream, *"Beyoncé,"* while ripping off my mask. Again, I'm *very* busy with my twenty-four hours as the queen of pop, soul, and R&B.

19. DENY BEING BEYONCÉ—There's nothing better than confusing people who are sure they know who you are by telling them, "No, but I get that all the time." I'd pull this shit all day long.

20. FOLLOW @TYLEROAKLEY ON TWITTER—This will actually have been the *first* thing I did on my day as Beyoncé. I would then make the hashtag #FollowTylerOakleyNow trend worldwide. This will be my legacy. I was here, world!

holy matriphony

EVERY WEDDING I'VE EVER ATTENDED HAS BEEN an absolute disaster. Sure, there must be some exceptions I'm forgetting, but the only one I can remember that wasn't the worst was a same-sex wedding in New York City. The gays were cute, the ceremony was intimate, the food was everything you'd hope for, and the drinks were flowing. That wedding was so good that they even slow-danced to the first minute of Lady Gaga's "Gypsy" as their first dance as a married couple, and when the tempo rose, invited all of their friends and family to booty-pop with them on the dance floor. I was a sobbing mess. And to think people thought we gays would ruin the sanctity of marriage.

Wait, hold that thought. If I remember correctly, after the reception we all went to a gay bar. I totally lost my black crushed-velvet blazer while my hands were down the front of stranger's pants. False alarm, yet another disaster for the records. Sorry, Billy and Pat, my personal misfortune lands your otherwise flawless matrimony into the flop category.

The first wedding I ever attended was my mom's second. She and my stepdad had always been cost-conscious, and their special day was no exception. The morning of the wedding, the six children from their combined previous failed marriages split into two groups, three of us picking up dog poop, while the other three were setting up lawn chairs on the uneven grass. It was to be a backyard wedding, with self-valet in the cul-de-sac.

I was six years old, and apparently on that day I "wasn't in the mood" to attend the wedding and "couldn't be bothered" to put on my tux. My parents had selfishly scheduled their wedding during the same time as the Mighty Morphin Power Rangers' second-season, two-part finale. How could they not respect that the Green Ranger, Tommy, had lost all of his powers and was about to come back as the White Ranger?! Unlike my mother's nuptials, this television event was unprecedented. Mom's second wedding? Essentially a rerun.

Unfortunately for me, my future-oldest-stepsister couldn't care less about my TV schedule. She picked me up by my shirt collar, came within an inch of my face, and snarled at me through clenched teeth about how, at the age of six, I needed to grow the fuck up. I learned a valuable lesson that day: if your mom is getting married, no excuse will get you out of attending the event—not even the biggest plot twist in Power Rangers history.

Since then, I've attended many weddings, but one of the best/worst was when I showed up to the wedding of a pair of strangers, and I was completely overdressed. Take a moment and imagine what that would even mean. Perhaps you're imagining a top hat, monocle, and cane? Or maybe a wedding dress of my own? Well, strangely, none of the above.

I was up in northern Michigan with my then-boyfriend Adam (see the chapter "The One That Got Away" for that shit-show), visiting for New Year's. Over the long weekend, I was told we'd be making a pit stop to attend a distant relative's New Year's Eve wedding. I packed what I thought was appropriate: a suit, complete with nice shoes, a cute shirt, a skinny tie—just your typical, basic wedding attire. Adam and I loved getting dressed up, and a wedding was sure to make us both cry—so we were pretty pumped for the ceremony, even if we didn't know the couple.

When we showed up to the address, I quickly realized this ceremony was going to be a lot more intimate than anticipated. It was a small cottage in the middle of a neighborhood, and although we double-checked the address, sure enough, this was it. We walked up to the front door and were greeted by the groom himself, ready for the biggest day of his life, in blue jeans and a T. Immediately feeling completely overdressed, I began to sweat. They say it's better to be overdressed than underdressed, and I assume that's because while you're sweating it out either way, a suit jacket at least conceals the fact.

We were joined by about ten other guests, all dressed as if they were about to attend a garage sale. I made small talk with some strangers, but between having to act as if I were my closeted boyfriend's platonic college friend and having to explain why I was wearing a suit, I was getting a bit anxious. So I did what any eating-disorder-recovering stress eater would do: I excused myself and made my way to the kitchen. Ahh, yes, food: my +1 for any event, my accomplice in any getaway. A full plate of cheese cubes, a few half-frozen shrimps, and a pile of tiny BBQ wieners to stuff my mouth with—nobody would find me unfrightening, much less approachable. I took my plate of snacks to the dining room, where I spent a conspicuous amount of time staring at a display case of collectible baby spoons. Then I moved on to repeat the tactic with a display case of collectible thimbles. I was the life of this party.

After killing some time hiding in the bathroom and staring at myself in the mirror, I flushed the unused toilet, fakewashed my hands, and opened the door to rejoin the party. My boyfriend, Adam, approached me with disbelief in his eyes. We both had thought we were attending a traditional wedding, maybe at a church, and definitely with at least a hundred guests we could blend in with. Instead, he told me the ceremony was about to start in the living room, and we were about to serve as witnesses.

We made our way in and took a seat in a La-Z-Boy love seat. Adam reached to pull the side lever to put up his footrest, and I slowly turned my head, wide-eyed, as if to communicate,

Have some respect, we are at a wedding-ish. He let go of the lever and sat up straight, stifling a laugh.

It was New Year's Eve, 11:00 p.m., when a man put down his beer and stood up to ordain the wedding. Nothing about the ceremony seemed planned, and the groom even interrupted the "ceremony" a few times to chitchat with a man in a plastic, inflatable chair across from me. I was baffled by the blasé attitude toward it all, but more than that, jealous of the bride's sweatpants.

When it was time for the vows, the bride and the groom threw their final curveball: an utterly romantic and personal set of promises to each other. They held each other's hands and looked into each other's eyes, tears streaming down their cheeks while expressing their most personal affections. I sat in my recliner, holding in my sniffles while tears dripped onto my suit. I finally saw the situation as it was intended: no glitz or glam, just pure love. It was their closest friends and family, no more, no less, plus two gays. The ceremony was never meant to wow anyone or conform to expectations. It was a promise of love, plain and simple. I wept and stuffed my face with BBQ wieners.

After the ceremony, Adam and I said our congratulations and good-byes before departing. We walked in silence down the sidewalk, and I reached out to hold Adam's hand as the snow fell silently on the sidewalk around us. The moment we got into Adam's car, we burst into laughter, speechless over how the night had gone. As Adam drove, I sat in silence, smiling while thinking about how when I got married someday, I could make my own rules too. If people got uncomfortable with how I celebrated my love, that was on them. Also, a bride in sweatpants? I bow down.

Years later, when I was living in San Francisco, I dated a guy named Danny. He was a journalist living in the East Bay, and every date we went on, I took the BART for forty minutes to see him. He was funny, charming, talkative, and challenged my way of thinking. I liked him. The first couple dates we went on, I'd ride the train with a book on my lap, watching the scenery through the windows, wondering if this was something I could do long term. Turns out, it wasn't, and we ended up fizzling out after a few months. All good, it happens. Afterward we saw each other every once in a while, usually at the Lookout when our respective groups of friends attended karaoke night. We generally kept to ourselves, but we were definitely cordial.

A couple months later, I got a text from him, completely out of the blue. *Hey! You in town next weekend?*

Yep! What's up? I replied.

Do you remember my cousin's wedding I mentioned having to go to? So . . . I don't have a date, wanna be my +1? I weighed my options as another text from him came through. *No pressure or expectations, obviously, and it's open bar. Come. It'll be fun. I'll get you drunk.*

I did enjoy free alcohol. . . . . *Sure, just let me know what to wear,* I replied, wary of overdressing.

Danny picked me up the afternoon of the wedding, and we caught up on the drive there. I glanced over at him as he drove. His eyes were on the road, and he smiled as he told a story. He was charming and handsome, and he caught me staring.

I looked away and adjusted my tie in the mirror. Hanging out with someone you kind of broke things off with for no concrete reason is weird—you start to rethink why y'all stopped talking in the first place, and whether getting together could mean *getting back together.*

That night at the wedding, Danny was the perfect date—he introduced me to everyone, made sure I always had a drink, and asked what songs I wanted him to request from the DJ. He treated me like a boyfriend. Is this what it would have been like had we stayed together? I watched him socialize at the next table over. At five feet four inches, he barely had to hunch while talking to a seated elderly couple. He was warm and kind with them, and adorable. He looked up, and we caught each other's eyes. He winked and I blushed.

"Okay, honestly, you guys are *too much!*" said his sister, sitting next to me, observing the interaction. "When's it going to be your turn?" She spun her finger to indicate the wedding.

"Oh, Lord," I groaned, "don't even say that." I laughed. Hers was the reaction we were getting from most of the wedding attendees. Though it was flattering, I did feel a little weird. Not once did Danny correct anybody and say that we were just friends.

"I think people think we're together," I whispered to Danny, while the best man gave his toast.

"Let them. Let's pretend we are. It'll be fun." Danny's hand was on my lower back.

A little smitten, I obliged.

Not until I met Danny's mom did I realize I was in too deep.

"So this is the Tyler you've been telling me about!" she said. "I was wondering when I was going to meet you."

I tilted my head and narrowed my eyes at Danny. He laughed nervously and asked who needed a refill. People weren't just incorrectly assuming. This little fucker was behind people's thinking we were together.

As he walked away with a few cups, I continued chatting with Danny's mom and began cautiously investigating just how misinformed the family was about our relationship. Just then, a few of Danny's cousins, whom I had met earlier, took the microphone drunkenly.

"Thank you all for coming and helping us celebrate our beautiful cousin's wedding," they said to applause. "Now we're all wondering which cousin is going to be next . . . Mason?" They pointed at one of Danny's cousins who was sitting alone at his own table drinking, clearly still single. He put up his hands in surrender, shaking his head. The crowd laughed.

"Maybe . . . Danny? And his special friend over there?"

Suddenly, all eyes were on us. My face went completely red, and I was now positive that my presence at the wedding was no fluke. My invitation to be his +1 was no out-of-the-blue text. This was a *trap*.

"We need to talk," I whispered to Danny, as his cousins dropped the microphone and left the stage. "What did you tell–" A pair of hands gripped my shoulders and I let out a yelp.

"Danny, do you mind if we steal this one for a few?" a cousin asked. I fixed a steely gaze on Danny. "We just wanna ask him some questions and get to know him a little better," another cousin followed up. My stare bore into my date. If he let the cousins take me, I was done for. This would be the end of me.

"Don't be too rough with him!" Danny laughed.

My jaw dropped as I was practically lifted out of my seat and guided out of the banquet hall. It was me and about seven or eight of Danny's most intimidating cousins. They were straight, masculine, and muscled, and under any other circumstances I would have quickly volunteered as tribute to be taken into a private room with them. As we went through the front doors and into the hallway, I looked over my shoulder and caught one last glimpse of Danny, cringing. He was dead to me.

The men brought me into an empty room with a bunch of chairs stacked against the wall. The cousin who seemed to be the oldest took a chair from the top of the stack and placed it in the middle of the room, as another took me by the shoulders and guided me to have a seat, firmly plopping me down. The men circled me. For years I had prayed for something like this, so I guess you should be careful what you wish for?

"So, what are your intentions with our baby cousin?"

My heart raced. Everyone was clearly under the impression that not only were Danny and I still dating, but we were getting serious. I looked around at all the men staring down at me from above, and I realized just how out of place Danny was in this group of cousins. He was tiny compared to them, far from athletic, and most notable of all was the only (openly) gay one of the bunch.

"We're taking it slow and just figuring things out. My intention is to treat him with respect." I was sweating. The cousins exchanged looks among themselves, seemingly pleased with my answer.

The next cousin took his turn. "Have you ever cheated on Danny?"

"No," I answered without a moment of hesitation. That was easy, because I hadn't. Maybe I could get through this interrogation without having to stretch the truth or spin my answers too much? Maybe if the rest of the questions were as simple, I could get out of this unscathed?

"Do you love Danny?"

I choked. Of course my answer was no, but do I tell them the truth and humiliate Danny, or do I bite the bullet and protect his dignity? My heart ached for him. He clearly was the perpetual bachelor of the family, and since he'd never been one to bring a +1 before, he obviously talked me up to just about everyone, maybe even innocently while we were still dating. I gave him the benefit of the doubt and imagined him, helpless, unable to get out of bringing this amazing, charming, handsome, hilarious, and above all, humble guy he had promised to the wedding. How could I blame him?

"I care about him deeply, and if I'm going to tell someone that I love him, he's going to hear it from me first—not from anyone who forced it out of me."

The cousin who asked narrowed his eyes at me, and I didn't break eye contact. He slowly nodded and looked to the next cousin. I exhaled.

After a few more questions, I found I had survived the interrogation. The cousins, pleased with my answers, pulled me up and brought me into a great big manly group hug. They ruffled my hair and playfully patted me on the back, and it was the closest I ever came to that "Fratguys Whip Out a Ruler" erotic story so formative to my budding sexual imagination.

I got back to the table where Danny sat with one arm

around his mom's shoulders. As I sat across from him, he looked at me.

I will kill you, I mouthed.

Sorry, he mouthed, before quickly downing his drink.

Just then, "My Humps" by the Black Eyed Peas began, and his mom screamed and frantically looked around the table for someone to dance with. When nobody volunteered, I grinned. I was never going to see these people again, and if I was going to be the best +1 of all time, why not go all out? I got up, took her hand, and led her to the empty dance floor, a move that was met by applause from the entire reception. I spun her around, sang along with every lyric, and couldn't care less that I was a sweaty mess. I looked back at Danny.

He sat, leaning back with his arms crossed, shaking his head. *I will kill you,* he mouthed.

Sorry, I replied, twirling away.

if you can't beet 'em

I'M PASSIONATE ABOUT THE CHEESECAKE FACTORY. So much so that I once threatened a man's life at one. But before you just assume I'm some type of middle-American mall-dining lunatic, let me explain.

The Cheesecake Factory is just one of those places where dreams come true. Free bread at the start of the meal . . . sides of spicy mayo handily available . . . unlimited refills on Diet Cokes that were already the size of my head . . . I guess I've always considered it some type of earthly heaven. It's where I celebrated the night I won two Teen Choice Awards in 2014, and where I took my mom out to dinner immediately after we were on *The Ellen Show* in 2015—it's sacred. When I grew up in mid-Michigan, the closest Cheesecake Factory was a four-hour drive away, and I always perceived it as a fancy restaurant, like California Pizza Kitchen or Olive Garden. Clearly, I'm a foodie.

My order at the Cheesecake Factory is simple. I always order the SkinnyLicious Veggie Burger—it's a patty consisting of a delicious blend of lentils, grains, and beets, topped with onions, tomatoes, cheese, avocado, and spicy mayo. It's fricking delicious—pardon my language. It's so fricking delicious, I *always* suggest it to newcomers to the establishment. It's compatible with almost all dietary restrictions, yet still edgy and fun, with a kick of beets that will make your shit a deep red the entire next day. What's not to love?

Now, don't get me wrong, I appreciate a restaurant that takes the time to create an entirely separate menu dedicated to healthy options. But if I had to make one complaint about the Cheesecake Factory, it would be the name they chose for this menu. If I didn't already have a complete lack of shame, I'd have a tough time as a grown man saying out loud to another adult that I'd take the "SkinnyLicious" version of anything. Luckily, the waiters of the Cheesecake Factory have to wear an entirely white outfit from head to toe, even out of season. We each have something to be ashamed of, to which we can tacitly agree to turn a blind eye.

I'm a man of routine. I enjoy the finer things in life, repeated over and over, until I've grown disgusted by them. On the scale of delightfully-just-discovered to absolutely-sick-of-it, I was somewhere around always-needing the SkinnyLicious Veggie Burger. Now, I'm by no means a vegetarian—Lord knows I'd deep-fry any animal and dip it in ranch dressing with absolutely zero hesitation or regrets. Now that I'm thinking about it, that sounds like a YouTube challenge. Stay tuned. So, yeah, that SkinnyLicious Veggie Burger . . . I love it on its own (coincidentally vegetarian) merits.

Sometime around mid-January in 2014, I was dining at

the Cheesecake Factory in the Grove outdoor shopping mall in West Hollywood, Los Angeles. I was joined by my friend Korey and his mom and brother, neither of whom I'd before had the pleasure of sharing a meal with. In an attempt to impress them with both my pseudo-health-consciousness and exotic tastes, I passionately recommended the Skinny-Licious Veggie Burger to Korey's brother. I couldn't say enough good things about it, and I told him how he would *die* for the beets in it. Like any levelheaded human, he was sold, and he ordered his own. Two SkinnyLicious Veggie Burgers coming our way! I felt like a missionary bringing the Good News to pagans. How could anyone be deprived of such glory? With so much beauty in this burger, it felt impossible that people could live their entire lives without knowing how blessed we are to be living contemporaneously with its wide and ready availability.

After a couple rounds of the free bread, our meals arrived. *This looks different,* I thought, and upon the first bite, I immediately realized what was wrong. No . . . beets?! I hadn't realized that the Cheesecake Factory had *another* veggie burger option, and Korey's brother's burger had the same defect! What happened to our beets?! I'd promised him an alarmingly red bowel movement coming the next day, and here I was, disappointing my guest. I was devastated.

I'm not one to ever send a meal back to the kitchen, not because I feel that it's rude, but because I've worked in food service with terrible human beings. I've seen teenage food preparers do unspeakable things to food for absolutely *no* reason, much less a merely flimsy one. I'm not saying bad things would necessarily have happened had I sent back my SkinnyLicious Veggie Burger, but I always like to play it safe.

Disappointed, I went home and had a completely unmemorable shit the next day. Save your pity for now, it gets worse.

Fast-forward a week. I was with a few of my YouTube friends at my apartment, playing bartender and making drinks. We couldn't decide what to do—it was Friday night, and everyone had a different notion of what an ideal night would look like. As a natural leader, it struck me how I could appease the masses . . . let's do tonight *right*. I looked at my boys with a smirk, knowing my next two words would elicit the most passionate consensus democracy had ever seen . . . *Cheesecake Factory*. I must have had one too many whiskey sours because I had completely forgotten the debacle of just one week prior. We hopped in a cab and headed down the street, with growling stomachs and dreams of outrageous portions, plus unlimited carbs and carbonation.

After perusing the absurd forty-page menu, I decided to just stick with my go-to choice: the SkinnyLicious Veggie Burger. As the waiter went around the booth taking our orders, one by one, I flashed back to the traumatic memory of what had happened last time: a *beetless* burger. This would *not* be happening again, so help me *God*. I asked the waiter tentatively, "So . . . the SkinnyLicious Veggie Burger . . . it says in the menu that it has beets in it, but last time—"

"Oh, yeah, they changed that, like, two weeks ago, it doesn't have beets anymore."

You know when someone tells a character in a movie or a TV show the most traumatic news, and the camera starts to slowly tilt and lose focus, the messenger's voice starts to soften and echo, and the recipient of the news stares off into the distance contemplating how life will never be the same? For me, this was that moment.

I snapped back into reality. "Fine . . . I'll take that . . . and a side of ranch." If I was going to be enduring a *beetless* burger, I'd at least drown my sorrows the only way I knew how. Twenty minutes later, I was completely sobered up, and there it was, a pale brown SkinnyLicious Veggie Burger, looking up at me as if to say, *Everything has changed.* I ate half, and I couldn't bring myself to take home the leftovers. Which had never before happened to me in my quarter century of life.

Now, I know you're thinking: *Tyler—there are worse things in the world. There are people who don't even have burgers.* I get that, and I validate their troubles. But let me be insane for a couple more pages, okay?

The next incident was mid-February, a full month after the initial menu change. I was checking into my hotel on a five-day trip to Hawaii. I was accompanied by a bunch of YouTube friends, who, while driving from the airport to the hotel, exclaimed in complete astonishment, "Look! They have a Starbucks here too!" "Oh my *God*! McDonald's!" All of us had completely forgot that we hadn't actually left the country. I guess it was our concept of the island's being isolated that also gave me the hope that maybe . . . just maybe . . . the Hawaiian Cheesecake Factory might be outdated, in the best way possible. There was only one way to find out.

After a long day at Waikiki Beach on the coast of Oahu, we

decided to return to the soft touch of a familiar friend, and we asked for a booth for four at the nearest Cheesecake Factory. While scanning the menu, I recounted to my friends my previous month of disappointments. I decided to ask the waiter if Oahu's SkinnyLicious Veggie Burger might—just might—still be made the old way . . . beets and all. In full confidence, our waiter assured me that it was still the same old SkinnyLicious Veggie Burger, made completely as stated in the menu . . . *beets and all!* I wanted it. I needed it. I ordered it, and I decided, fuck, it's been a month of disappointment, I'm not even going to get it SkinnyLicious—*add cheese! Let's get crazy!* Beets are the perfect reason to throw my SkinnyLicious diet right out the window. In fact, give me an order of deep-fried macaroni-and-cheese balls for the whole table. Let's get fucking *nuts*. When my friends ignore potential partners' negative qualities because of how hot they are, I describe them as blinded by the beauty. In this same way, I was blinded by the beets. I didn't give any fucks. I was ready.

As time went on, my lust for the beets grew, and my doubts about their availability began to take root. What if the waiter didn't know about the change? It's the exact same menu, and it's a chain restaurant . . . and, I mean, we *are* still in America . . . technically. This might not end well. No, no, no . . . don't be silly. I had asked the waiter; he confirmed the beets would come. It's as simple as that. I need to trust him. Our waiter *gets* me. He knows how important this is to me—how important it is *period*.

Then the food started to arrive. One by one, my friends received their plates of outrageous portions, until I was the last one without any food. My eyes shifted from plate to plate. My thoughts began to race—this is it. This is the moment he comes over and tells me there's been a mistake. No, no, no . . . it's coming. It's coming. It must be coming.

"I swear to God, if my burger doesn't have beets in it—" I began, right as our waiter rounded the corner empty-handed. Our eyes met, and I knew. Last time, my body involuntarily resorted to shock. This time, something different happened.

"So I just checked with the kitchen, and unfortun—"

Boom.

You know that urban legend about the mom who gets in a car accident, and her baby is stuck underneath a car, and in this urgent situation her body gives her enough adrenaline to lift the car and save the baby? And afterward, she comes to and realizes she blacked out and doesn't recall anything that happened? That was me at the Cheesecake Factory that day. I blacked out in a rage fueled by absent beets. As the waiter scurried back to the kitchen, I began to regain my senses. My friends gawked at me, and I began to laugh nervously. Wait . . . what did I just say to him? Did I make a fool of myself? Was I an asshole? Like, more than usual?

They recounted everything that had happened just two minutes earlier, and I was appalled. Apparently, in a fit I couldn't control, I had slammed my fists on the table, sneering, as these words came out of my mouth: *"I will fucking kill someone."* I wasn't loud enough to be heard by any other tables, but I was loud enough to definitely get me escorted out if I weren't a five-foot-five-inch, platinum-blond twink in a tank top. *"Fine, bring me the normal Veggie Burger. That's fine. I don't fucking care."*

I had been blinded by the beets. I had threatened to kill

someone over a SkinnyLicious Veggie Burger. If I hadn't had my T-Mobile incident back in high school, this would have been my official all-time low.

When our waiter returned, he was accompanied by his manager, and I knew this was to be the most shameful moment of my life: I'd be escorted out of the Cheesecake Factory while on vacation in Hawaii for threatening to end the life of a man in an all-white outfit and nonslip white shoes. I deserved it. I'd crossed a boundary, and that simply doesn't fly at a classy restaurant such as the Cheesecake Factory. I looked at my friends with an expression that communicated my apologies for being the source of their embarrassment, then I looked up at the employees who would now be putting me in my place.

"About the beet situation . . ."

Oh, great, now this has become a *situation*. Our waiter totally went back and told everyone he had a *situation* on his hands. And it's me, I'm the situation. He's going to go home today and get on Skype and talk to his girlfriend, whom he's in a long-distance relationship with, and complain to her about me, and she'll tell him to not let it bother him, because I'm just a low-life, shitty person who doesn't care about anyone but himself, and also she thinks they should start seeing other people. I was sure of it.

My head dropped, my hands were clasped under the table to ensure no more slamming fists, and just as I was ready to be taken away to my unfortunate fate, the manager surprised me: "We are very sorry, and because of the mix-up, we're going to give you your meal free."

Who *was* this man? Why was he forgiving me my sins?

What did I do to deserve a second chance? In the words of our good friend Jesus Christ, homeboy got slapped and turned the other cheek. Side note: I am unfamiliar with the Bible, but I'm assuming it was Jesus who said that?

God, I'm a fucking dick. That's all I could think. It was a simple misunderstanding, yet somehow I forgot that the waiter just made an honest mistake. He didn't mean to deprive me of my beets. As someone who has been on the other side of the service counter, how could I be so blind to the situation and treat him like that? Well, if you'd ever had the original version of the SkinnyLicious Veggie Burger, you'd understand. But still.

I apologized profusely to the waiter for the fit that I threw, and he assured me that it was okay. As if the free meal weren't enough, he told me I could also have my choice of free cheesecake. In my shame, it tasted like ashes, but that didn't stop me from finishing it.

mood killer

TYPICALLY, I WON'T BE CAUGHT DEAD ON A beach. There's just something about the texture of sand, the inescapable dampness of the ocean, and the unappealing possibility of being eaten by a shark. And, yes, I know, you have more of a chance of being struck by lightning than being bitten by a shark, but I'll pass on both.

So when I was in Hawaii for a YouTube convention in early 2014, I was definitely a bit out of my element. Luckily, the men there were enough to distract me from my objections and lure me to the sand, and, boy, was I on the prowl. They were tall, tan, and their muscles bulged from surfing. In contrast, I was pale, dumpy, and likely to hiss like a raccoon at the mere mention of physical activity. I could only hope the locals would find our differences exotic and intriguing.

And one did! We met on Grindr and decided to meet up in the lobby of my hotel, then go for a walk on the beach. So there I sat, on a bench next to the bellhop, with him knowingly judging me for what I was obviously doing in the lobby at 2:00 a.m. When my guy arrived, he was just as handsome as his pictures, and I was all heart-eyes emoji. We made our way to the empty beach, where just twelve hours ago swarms of tourists had been. The moon was huge, the crashing waves were the only sound, and I was thirsty.

We moseyed down the damp beach, flip-flops dangling from our fingers, chatting about who we were, what we wanted to do with our lives, and everything in between. At first he was shy and quiet, but also incredibly handsome with a perfect smile. He told me about his family and his job as a teacher, and I told him about the weird life I had as a YouTuber. Sometimes I can be forward, but this guy seemed so gentle, unassuming—and a little bit nervous—that I let him take the lead. As we walked, the backs of our hands brushed against each other a few times, until he finally made a move and grabbed mine into his.

"I'm glad we met up," he said.

"Me too."

As we walked in silence, still holding hands, I thought about how different our lives were. For the average person, you're in one place, you get to know someone, you go on some dates, and it either turns into something or doesn't. Here I was, traveling constantly, with one night to share with each guy I met. My spirits sank, thinking about how this great guy was here with me, but I'd be saying good-bye and flying home the next day. Out of instinct, I squeezed his hand three times, and then I was flustered when I realized what I had done. During the early days of my relationship with my college boyfriend, he would hold my hand and squeeze three times, as if to say, *I like you.* I'd return his squeezes with four, replying *I like you too.* I guess I liked this guy.

After a few more minutes of walking on the sand, he stopped, looked over at me, and for the first time held steady eye contact. His eyes were huge and brown, and I was sure he was mustering up the courage to kiss me. He smiled, my heart raced, and just then, in an act of homophobic divine intervention, a flashlight swept our direction. God is so rude sometimes.

We turned and squinted in the direction of whoever was holding the flashlight, and we realized it wasn't pointed at us, but instead about thirty feet in front of us. Something dark was in the sand. As we slowly moved toward it, my Hawaiian took my hand again, and I could tell he was nervous. Step by step, I held his hand tighter, unsure of what this motionless thing was, and even more unsure as to why we were approaching it.

"Oh my God," my date whispered, as we both realized simultaneously what it was.

Nothing ruins the mood of a Grindr date quite like finding a human corpse. As we approached, we realized the people with flashlights were police. As we were escorted away from the scene, we heard hushed whispers about a shark attack. Spooked by the thought of having my beautiful feet eaten, I stepped far away from the tide and insisted we go back up to the sidewalk.

Friends and family, if you're reading this on a beach towel with the smell of sunscreen in the air and sand between your toes, wondering why I said "No thank you" to your invitation to accompany you on this beautiful afternoon in the sun, now you know. The reason I'll never be caught dead on a beach is because I literally don't want to be caught dead on a beach.

Back to my date. Our romantic moment had been snuffed

out, so I brushed off the sand and stepped back into my flip-flops.

"We should have taken a selfie with the body," he joked. I was relieved at his effort to lighten the mood after such a jarring experience. It was the kind of gallows humor I would hope for in a kindred spirit.

"But how could we pick a filter that would work for all three of us?" I asked.

He laughed, took my hand, and we made our way back to my hotel. In front of the lobby, he stopped, turned toward me, and took hold of both of my hands.

"Thanks for tonight. Sorry about the corpse," he said.

I said nothing, but I did squeeze his hands three times.

Side note: a year and a half later, my Hawaiian happened to be in Seattle the same night I was in town for my Slumber Party Tour. He came to the show, was bewildered by the experience, we went out to the gay bars afterward, and he came over to spend the night. Nothing crazy happened, but he did puke in my bed from being too drunk. Thanks for tonight. Sorry about the puke.

the apple doesn't fall far

MY PARENTS HAVE BEEN DIVORCED AND remarried to other people for as long as I can remember. Technically, I come from what the media might call "a broken home," but I just always assumed everyone's family was as bizarre and dysfunctional as mine. Between my parents and stepparents, my family tree is a tangled mess— but I wouldn't have it any other way.

A quick note to my parents: *While I've been writing this book, nobody in my life has expressed more anxiety about the stories I'll tell than the four of you. It's as if you thought your son would never have the opportunity to write a book and expose you, so you just lived and did whatever you pleased. Well, hi! I wrote a book! Please enjoy this chapter!*

I don't have any memories of my mom and dad enjoying each other's company, but I do have distinct memories of their hating each other. From an early age, I had severe anxiety anytime my parents had to be within one hundred feet of each other. Parent-teacher conferences meant armpit sweat down to my rib cage. Soccer games meant binge-eating doughnut holes and chugging Capri Suns to distract myself from seeing them near each other on the sidelines. Knowing my dad was in my mom's driveway to pick me up for visitation every Tuesday and every other weekend made me feel like I could puke. Even fifteen years later, at the Michigan stop of my Slumber Party Tour, seeing them in the same audience made me feel like I might have diarrhea onstage in my onesie. It's strange to me that they might once have been in love, but allegedly they were.

My parents were high school sweethearts. My mom attended Catholic school, while my dad went to public school. They got knocked up while they were still in high school, and they gave the baby up for adoption.* They got married after high school and started their life together by having two more kids: my sister Codi and me. Soon after, they got divorced, which to this day is still a sticky, messy situation riddled with he-said, she-said, he-did, she-did. All I know is that no happy marriage

---

* Twenty-one years later, that sister of mine that I was told about but thought I'd never meet called our house. She was raised about fifteen minutes away from us. Small, crazy world.

ends in divorce, and I'm grateful that they were able to move on to the next chapters in their lives.

What made the biggest impact on me was having two separate homes with two separate sets of parents. Between the strange parenting habits of all four of them, it's a wonder that I'm able to interact with other humans, let alone go out in public. It's not that they didn't raise me well: let's just say that they had a lot of . . . quirks.

My mom is my favorite human on earth, despite that she farts nonstop. Not until recently did I finally convince her to stop farting in the house and to start farting out of the sliding door to the back porch.

She's caring, compassionate, warm, and funny, and she always puts her kids and grandkids first. She makes the best manicotti and creates her own greeting cards in her craft room downstairs. I'm her favorite, so that makes me like her more too. When I was growing up, she and my stepdad owned a craft store called Papa Woody's Woodshop.* My stepdad would

---

* I have no clue who Papa Woody is, and if it's meant to be my stepdad, that's the strangest self-appointed nickname I've ever heard.

make benches and hutches and chairs and tables, and my mom would make seasonal scrunchies. My mom had a scrunchie store, which eventually burned to the ground, apparently due to an accident involving a soldering iron and a bundle of hay.

In my mom's eyes, I can do no wrong. Once I was so mad at her for some reason that I gave her the middle finger during a family dinner, and all my brothers laughed at me and my mom rolled her eyes. I was so embarrassed. She's been to jail for a reason she refuses to tell me, and she has a floral tramp-stamp tattoo that she got on spring break a few years ago. She's called the Queen for a reason.

My favorite thing I got from my mom is an ability to be authentically myself, no matter the circumstances. She doesn't change for anyone, and I don't either—for better or for worse. My least favorite thing I got from her is the tendency to take everything personally—and I *can't wait* to hear what she took personally in this book.

My stepdad is a free spirit. By that, I mean I usually had to call home to make sure he wasn't naked before I invited friends over. He's patient and analytical and has always encouraged me to be myself. Growing up, he taught me most of my life lessons, like how if you put a towel up against the front door, the air-conditioning won't escape during the summer—or that milk is usually fine to drink a few days past its expiration date. Most of his clothes have holes in them, and he's got stacks of coupons and receipts sticking out of his pockets. He sets every clock fast, but can't keep track which clocks are ahead by which amounts. When he texts, he always signs off with an acronym he made up and assumes everyone uses, LYB NBC—which means "love ya, babe; nuts, back & critters"—the first half being pretty self-explanatory. Less obviously, "nuts, back, and critters" means watch out for crazy people, watch your back because you can't trust anyone, and don't run over any animals. It's a wonder this lingo hasn't caught on among tweens on Twitter.

My stepdad never quite understood my interests, but he always supported them. When I was obsessed with Pokémon, he made me a wooden caddy for my deck, and he let me skip school the day the movie came out, so I could see it in a theater. It was the cinematic event of my lifetime, and he was next to me snoring.

Seeing a movie with my stepdad is an experience. He's incredibly frugal and will smuggle in an entire meal. Once, while rifling through his pocket looking for his ticket stub, a cheeseburger fell out of his shirt and onto the theater floor. He will loudly open bags of chips, crinkle hamburger foil, and open soda cans with no regard for the rest of the audience. He has poor hearing and will lean over to ask what's happening—not once, but throughout the entire movie. One time he didn't like a movie, so after watching the entire two hours, he went to the reception desk to politely ask for his money back—and got it.

You'll always know if my stepdad is approaching because he walks around with his phone in his shirt pocket, blasting Native American flute music at all times of the day. He loves Dolly Parton and insists she's one of the greatest humans to ever live. He's a hard worker and a great father. I once accidentally hit him in the face with a racquet at the YMCA, and he never once blamed me as blood was gushing from his eye. The older I get, the more I like him.

My favorite thing I got from him is the phrase "Friends come and friends go, but family is forever"—which I understand more deeply each and every year. My least favorite thing I got from him is a cavalier disregard for expiration dates on perishable foods.

My stepmom has always been a bit kooky. My dad met her while we were apartment searching, and he tells me that I pointed out one complex as we were driving by. He turned into the parking lot and met her at the reception desk. They fell in love and got married. After two decades of marriage, they ended up getting divorced this past year, but I still love her to pieces.

I'm obsessed with how my stepmom is so strange, but yet she is 100 percent aware and embraces every bit of it. She is hilarious, energetic, passionate, and bizarre, and she's in on her own joke. She sneaks into closets to chug energy drinks and giggles if anyone catches her. She calls the toilet "the twirlet." She's instilled in me a fear of miscellaneous food mishaps, telling me at a young age that a worm could likely be sucked up through the straw of my juice box, and that ants often colonized cereal boxes. To this day, I can't raid the pantry without thinking of her.

She is religious, but she will never pick a fight with anyone over it. Her current favorite product is a service that automatically filters out anything inappropriate from movies. I recently checked their website, and they have thousands of titles to choose from, all free of cuss words and any premarital hand-holding.

My favorite thing I got from her is a carefree spirit. My least favorite thing I got from her is using substitutes for censored words—such as "Sugar fudge!" if I stub my toe. Somehow, that sounds dirtier than what I might have said in the first place?

My dad is a simple guy who got better as the years went on. When I was younger, I hated him and made his life a living hell by being a little shit. For example, I once told my mom shortly after their divorce that I saw my dad drinking and driving, failing to mention it was a Diet Coke. I was a difficult child, and he responded by unhinging my bedroom door and removing it as punishment. For decades, we were two bulls that locked horns. Add in the homophobia and it all got ugly.

As a kid, I was always arguing with my older sister, Codi. My dad's chosen punishment was timed hugs with both of us inside one oversize T-shirt. We'd hold each other in our arms, angrily, and my dad would cackle at the sight of both of our heads poking out of an XXXL T. He'd make up over-the-top compliments that we'd have to repeat to each other, face-to-face. We'd start furious at each other, but we always ended up in fits of laughter.

Throughout our childhood, my dad made the entire family do a series of family photos where we were stacked one on top of the other, something all of us dreaded.

He tried his best and put up with a lot of my bullshit. Unfortunately, when all the coming-out stuff happened, our relationship went sour. For a few years in my early twenties, we didn't speak at all. We've moved past that now. He's apologized and acknowledged that he was an idiot, and I've accepted his apology. I love getting together with him, and I think of him as more of a buddy than my dad. We get together for a few beers (he only drinks Michelob Ultra), he talks through his women troubles, I talk through my guy troubles, and we get drunk and giggly. After years of butting heads, we've found something that works for us, and I'm pretty happy with that.

A weird thing happens when you grow up and suddenly you're an adult—and the dynamic between parent and child shifts. My dad and I recently went through that, and I think it was what saved our relationship. He always told me that he regretted not having a relationship with his own dad, who passed away before they were able to mend their problems. I'm glad we've gotten to a good place. Hopefully we've got plenty more years to go before one of us kicks it.

My favorite thing I got from him is his laugh. We have identical laughs. My least favorite thing I got from him is how red our faces get in response to literally anything, ever. I hope his reading this chapter didn't evoke his tomato face too much.

dream job

"**H**I, YOU PROBABLY DON'T REMEMBER ME, but five years ago I ruined your life."

This was the conversational opener of a man who approached me at the YouTube Creator Summit in April 2015. It was YouTube's tenth birthday, and they invited top creators from around the world to celebrate in New York City with parties, presentations, and intimate chats with Google executives. I looked at the guy in front of me, puzzled, trying to figure out what he did to me. Thinking back, the only thing I could recall to be devastating in 2010 was *The Oprah Winfrey Show* going into its final season. Was this his doing?!

He did look a bit familiar, and I tried to remember what went wrong at the start of my final year of college, and then suddenly it hit me. In 2010, I was twenty-one, about to graduate from Michigan State University, and couldn't secure a nine-to-five job for the life of me. I was applying for every opening and attending every job fair, but nothing seemed to stick.

The furthest I got with any of my applications was with Google. Having just been declared one of the best companies to work for, it was every graduate's dream job, and the competition was tough. Getting hired at Google is daunting. First, I applied with a set of referrals from other employees. Next, I had multiple phone screenings, in which I was asked just about every typical interview question. Google was famous for inserting a few creative "Googley questions" into interviews, and one that stuck out was how would I find a needle in a haystack? I knew the expected answers, like using a magnet or throwing the pile into a pool and watching the needle sink, or burning the haystack and finding the needle in the ashes, but my answer had to be a little more me. I declared that I'd throw a party and invite everyone I knew. At the end of the night, I'd have each attendee take one straw as they departed. In the morning, while nursing my hangover, I'd find my needle sitting there, exposed and untouched. My answer got me through to the next round of interviews.

I was then brought in for a mixer with dozens of other candidates. All the confidence I had built up from my phone screening came crumbling down when I saw just how talented my peers were. But in the same way a drag queen wins in *RuPaul's Drag Race*, I used my charisma, uniqueness, nerve, and talent to outshine the other prospective employees, and I advanced to the next stage.

I was more than three months into the hiring process when I came in for the final round of intense, full-day interviews at Google headquarters. I performed as best as I could, gave honest, thoughtful answers, and demonstrated my unparalleled enthusiasm for the position. Nothing was going to stand between me and my dream job—and my ability to finally pay my bills week to week without paralyzing fear. After the interviews, I went home to stay with my parents over Christmas break. Knowing that a decision was coming within the week, I refreshed my e-mail compulsively and checked my phone every second.

When I finally got the call, my crystal-clear vision of a perfect future at Google vanished into thin air. It was a simple no, with no reason attached. The caller thanked me for my time and wished me the best in my future endeavors. I sat, confused, feeling crushed and lost. I was buried deep in debt, so close to graduation, and so clueless about my career path, that I started to panic. I spent the next few months scrambling to find a job, but I had no luck.

Graduating college with zero prospects is simultaneously terrifying and freeing—on the one hand, I was embarrassed and poor and dreading my impending student-loan payments, and on the other hand, the possibilities of what I could do were endless. So, after donning my cap and gown to collect my diploma, I flew to San Francisco with my best friend, Korey, for a weekend getaway. On Saturday, we explored the city recklessly. We fell in love with the idea of leaving Michigan for a brand-new adventure. That afternoon, we saw an apartment for rent that was open to the public for viewing. We giggled as we stepped into the building near 16th and Castro, as if we were actually prospective renters, but we were soon quiet. We fell in convincing love with the listing and realized that the cost was doable. While browsing the empty rooms, we exchanged glances that communicated a shared madness. As thrilling as an elopement, without telling anyone, we signed the lease the next day. After our return flight to Michigan, we broke the news to our friends and family, and we packed our bags. I trusted that even though I had no job lined up, I had already exhausted the possibilities in Michigan. Why not try California?

After applying for literally every position posted on Craigslist: San Francisco, I scored an internship running social media and community management for a start-up. I had been doing it for years as a personal hobby on YouTube, so it felt like a good career fit as a young professional. Eventually, my position became full-time, and I began to carve my path in the digital workspace. It wasn't the perfect job, but I was able to pay my bills and explore a new city with new possibilities. Leaving Michigan for San Francisco introduced me to myself. I met new people, tried new things, and I was inspired to live and create like never before. My passion for YouTube became all-consuming.

As my online presence grew, so did my impatience at work. During the day, I'd struggle to influence my teams over the basics of social media management, how connections online happened in real time and relied on instinct. Every day was a new battle to get them to trust me. With so many hoops to jump through with campaigns and social posts, by the time they were approved, it was already too late. Then I'd come home to a life on YouTube where I was my own boss and able to create my own content without anyone restricting me.

I was so inspired to create, and so frustrated in the workplace, that I started to consider the possibility of pursuing You-

Tube as a full-time career. I was getting more views than ever before, and I was finally bringing in a tiny income through my YouTube channel that could, if maintained, pay my rent. So, trusting the same instincts that brought me to San Francisco in the first place, I quit my office job to pursue a full-time job as a YouTuber. And it worked.

Getting rejected by the dream job at Google gave me the freedom to pursue something I never thought was even possible. I'd wanted to work at Google in the first place not because I had a passion for sales or because I furiously hated Bing or AskJeeves; rather, I was told that that's what my aspiration *should* be. Only when I failed to get *the* dream job was I able to figure out *my* dream job.

For years, I never knew why I didn't get that position at Google back in 2010, and the question was always in the back of my head. Fast-forward to 2015, at the YouTube Creator Summit. A man came up to me to remind me of that time when he destroyed all of my hopes and dreams. This guy wasn't responsible for taking *Oprah* off the air, he was my final interviewer during my three-month-long pursuit of "the dream job."

"When everyone at Google wanted to hire you, I was the one guy who said *absolutely not*. You were too creative, and as much as you were the perfect fit for Google, Google wasn't the perfect fit for you."

My jaw dropped, and I couldn't help but laugh out loud at his story and the serendipity of the situation. There I was, having just met with Google executives, on the day that I was officially offered a national marketing campaign in which my face would be plastered all over subways and billboards across the country as an ambassador of YouTube. And I was talking to the man responsible for sending me down the path that got me to there in the first place.

Finding my dream job was like finding a needle in a haystack. It was a crazy party in which every failed path I followed was like an attendee required to take away a single straw of hay as they departed, one by one. It took a while, and I eventually found that needle, but I couldn't have done it without failing over and over.

The Google employee who saved me from an entirely different life pointed across the party to a gigantic portrait of my face that a squad of teens were taking selfies with.

"I think it all worked out," he said.

one direction

I FIRST DISCOVERED ONE DIRECTION WHILE LIVING in San Francisco. My time in SF was even more party-focused than my time in college, and my friends and I typically went to the bars Tuesday, Wednesday, Thursday, Friday, and Saturday evenings, and Sunday afternoons (even God rested on the seventh day).

At the time, I was living with my best friend, Korey, in the Castro, which is the gay neighborhood of the city, with most of SF's gay bars right in its heart. By that age, we knew what we wanted, and we wanted to be in the middle of it all. Our best friends were dispersed throughout the city, so our home became the meeting place for all things social. Every night at around 9:00 p.m., our buzzer rang with someone assuming we'd be going to the bars (correctly).

The buzzer was our cue to push play on "Korey's Jams," a playlist made with that week's yet-to-be-discovered hits. Korey was always on top of all the new music—he was blasting Chumbawamba long before other people's radios were pissing the night away. One fateful night in August of 2011, with a freshly updated playlist, Korey pressed play.

Up in my room, deciding which black-on-black-on-black outfit looked most slimming for that evening's festivities, I heard the opening chords of "Summer Nights," from the musical *Grease*. I didn't think anything of it and had no idea that my life was about to change forever. Having decided on my black, denim, short-sleeved button-down (different from last night's black, denim, long-sleeved button-down), I made my way downstairs to ask whoever just arrived if I looked lumpy.

Rounding the corner into our kitchen, I found one of our best San Francisco friends, LuLu. His real name was Laurence. He was thirty-one but told everyone he was in his early twenties. A Filipino with a thick accent that he played up for comedic effect, he loved to play dumb. He was petite, energetic, and flirtatious, and every phrase he spoke somehow came out as a flamboyant moan. He was somewhat of the Regina George of San Francisco—he knew everyone's business, and he could get us on the list for any event or in the door at any bar. He was one of the first friends I made in the city, and we immediately became attached at the hip.

"Oh my Gahhhhhhhhhhh, Tyler, you look so gooooooooood!" he reassured me, in between gasped screams of lyrics, while he danced in the kitchen. I had no clue what the song was, but LuLu was living—completely off-key. *"That's what makes you beau-tuh-ful!"*

"What song was that?" I asked, completely oblivious, and more interested in considering what I'd be drinking that night.

"*Goirl!* You dun know One Duhrection!? Oh no no no no no

no no no no no . . . this will not do . . . come look." He sat down on our counter, simultaneously pouring shots and pulling out his phone. "That one's Louis"—he did a shot—"he's the hot one."

"Zayn is the hot one," screamed Korey from downstairs.

"Show me Zayn," I insisted, trusting Korey's taste implicitly.

My fascination with these five delectable British boys was immediate. Their songs instantly joined our rotation of prebar songs—and they were a hit with me and all of my San Francisco gays. I was obsessed, and I felt like a pretween girl thirsty for the unobtainable. The 1D boys felt so distant, unreachable, monumentally famous—my online expressions of my love for them would grow to be playful and obnoxious, knowing they'd never see anything I was saying, nor would I ever have the chance of being in the same room as them.

In April of 2012, just a few months later, I got a call from LuLu, screaming about some contest that we had to enter and win. I had no idea what he was going on about, but after a little explanation, I got all the details: the boys had just announced on Twitter that their new DVD special of the Up All Night concert tour was coming soon, and as part of the promotion, they were sending advance copies of the DVD to their biggest fan accounts on Twitter, so that they could host their own viewing parties. This was one party LuLu could not get us into—it was up to me.

I applied, and by the grace of God, I was chosen! Soon after, I received my box of party favors (tickets to give to my friends, posters, stickers, temporary tattoos, etc.), but LuLu and I decided this simply wasn't enough, we wanted to go all out. We made our way to the grocery store and came across the magazine aisle. We picked up every magazine we could—*Tiger Beat, BOP, J-14, Twist*—any and *all* tween glossies that featured the boys of One Direction on the cover. I felt that if there was a way to stalk One Direction from an ocean away, this was it. Right then and there, it clicked. I bought the magazines, ran home after work, filmed myself flipping through the pages—half legitimately fangirling over the boys, half making fun of people like myself who fangirl over the boys. I uploaded "How to Stalk One Direction" to YouTube and went downstairs to set up for the party.

After a night of debauchery with a dozen of my closest gays, in which we made up drinking games based on the exclusive One Direction concert DVD (e.g., drink every time the boys can't dance), I drunkenly made my way up to my room. Snuggled up in my bed, I checked my YouTube channel to see how my new video was doing. The response was immediate and intense—unlike any other video I had ever uploaded.

To this point, I had never had a video go viral—contrary to how the public believes a YouTube star is born. Don't get me wrong, some find immediate success with a big viral hit, but that was never my situation. But this video . . . it was spreading in ways I had never even imagined. When the One Direction fandoms on Twitter and Tumblr discovered my creation, it spread like wildfire. The video was candid, spontaneous, and just me goofing around, but hundreds of thousands of teenage girls saw themselves in it.

Immediately, my Twitter and YouTube presence exploded, growing by tens of thousands a day, something I never thought possible. Five years into my YouTube career, I had found my calling—and it was speaking in the language of teenage fan-girls.

With this huge boost, my videos picked up steam, and I quickly realized that the demographic watching my content was shifting—younger and more fan-culture-oriented. Over time, I continued to deliver the videos I wanted to make, but I was unafraid to play with the direction (no pun intended) of the content itself.

Throughout 2013, so much of my brand warped and shifted to play along with the fandom culture surrounding One Direction, and I loved it. I loved being a part of such a passionate community every day. I tweeted as just another member of the fandom, excited for whatever that day's announcement or release was. I would live-tweet music-video releases. I had the boys' birthdays in my calendar with jokes drafted to tweet to them. My love for them and their music was authentic, and I had no shame about embodying the concept of a professional fangirl.

On Tuesday, July 23, 2013, I joined in on the discussion, a routine chat with the fandom. It was 9:00 a.m., and there I was, just having a coffee, browsing Twitter, the usual. That day, we were trying to break a Vevo record for number of views in twenty-four hours for a music video—a normal event for us—and to add my part, I tweeted, "You know what I've got on repeat? The #BestSongEver video. Let's break a record."

And then *bam*. It happened. Harry-fucking-Styles re-tweeted me. Not just a simple retweet though—no, *this guy* . . . he added his own flare. He manually retweeted my promo and added "Thanks mate!" to the end of it.

I screamed. I literally yelped. As it was happening, I started involuntarily giggling and decided, *No, I'm a vlogger, I have to record this moment and save it for eternity.* I calmly set up my tripod, turned on my camera, and then reacted. What came out of that four minutes of filming now lives in infamy on my YouTube channel.

Six days later, I got an e-mail from a rapper I had never heard of, offering me "the opportunity of a lifetime." The offer was simple: I was to attend the One Direction concert with him, where I would meet the boys, in exchange for promoting him and his music and publicly attending his show, where I had to say I was his fan. It felt dirty. Though I was obsessed with the boys and would have killed for the chance to meet them, I just couldn't do it like that. Bummed, I politely declined, knowing someday I'd meet them on my own terms, without compromising my integrity.

One week later, I got an e-mail that changed everything.

The e-mail asked if I would be interested in interviewing the boys during their first movie's press-junket day. This was my chance! I could finally sit across from Zayn and stare blankly for a few minutes before they asked me to leave!

After five minutes of discussing it on the phone, my answer was obvious: yes, yes, *YAAAAAAS*. I hung up, sat on my couch—the same exact spot where I sat when Harry Styles retweeted me, grinning. I couldn't believe it. The band I'd spent so much of my time and energy promoting and genuinely adoring? I might have the chance to meet them. The obvious next question was . . . oh, God, do I delete all the evidence of my thirst leading up to this point? No. Let it live. Thirst unashamedly, Tyler.

That month, I had just launched a project called Auguest, a monthlong collaboration series during August, with surprise special guests every single weekday. This is now an annual tradition, but the format during its first year in 2013 was simple: twenty YouTubers, twenty uploads. Upon launch, I had a list of YouTubers I hoped would participate, but not every spot was accounted for. After getting off the call, I realized . . . what if the interview was the finale for the month? During our next call, I proposed the idea of keeping the interview a secret and launching it on August 30. I was ready to make the Internet explode, but I had no idea how I was going to keep this secret.

Before getting the offer to interview the boys, I had actually planned on going to their LA show five days later with a crew of YouTubers. We sat in a box overlooking the entire stadium. Never missing an opportunity to self-promote, I was wearing my very own PROFESSIONAL FANGIRL T-shirt, which, prior to the show, felt appropriate. Upon arriving, I instantly regretted it—nothing said Tyler Oakley more than Tyler Oakley merch . . . except for Tyler Oakley wearing Tyler Oakley merch. I stuck out like a deer with lilac hair wearing his own merch. I peeked over the edge down to the seats below and was met with dozens of eyes glued to the box. *#spotted*

I leaned back in my chair, not wanting to make any sudden movements. What once was a constant buzz of excited chatter soon transformed into a slow and growing chant. I grasped the ledge in front of me, found my balance, and slowly stood, looking over the stadium. I rose to see the breathtaking view in front of me, coupled with the even more shocking sound accompanying it—thousands of teenage girls yelling in unison, *"TYLER, TYLER, TYLER."* I looked in disbelief at my friends around me, then back to the crowd, and with one sweeping motion waved to the people. An insane roar swept the stadium. Holy fuck.

I slumped to my seat, my face flushed and red, overwhelmed by the outpouring of emotion. These people had come to see the biggest boy band in the world, and while they waited for the main event, they made me feel like the opening act. Never in my wildest dreams did I ever imagine this would be my life.

Soon after, the lights dimmed, the concert began, and the boys delivered what all of us came to eat up—an unapologetically over-the-top teenybopper show worthy of one of the biggest stadiums in America. Even from all the way up and back, this performance was one to remember. I screamed along to every lyric until the very last song. I felt ready.

On August 23, I packed my bag and discreetly flew to New York City. I was undercover and refrained from my usual "New York City, I am in you" tweet to keep everything hush-hush. I told my driver the hotel name I saw in my itinerary, and as we rolled up to the destination, I saw dozens of teenage girls waiting outside the front door. I realized that this was probably the hotel the boys were staying at too, so as quickly as I could, I got out of the car and approached the front door. The crowd screamed as half of them recognized me as Tyler Oakley, and the other half thought I was Niall Horan. Shit. My cover was blown.

When I made it to my hotel room, it was already the middle of the night, and I was both exhausted and wide-awake. I lay under the covers, mind reeling about what was coming. In less than twenty-four hours, I'd be in the same room as the biggest band in the world—how was it going to turn out? Sure I could ask them the safe, mundane questions they always get asked . . . or I could do something different. I thought about the digital age we live in, where the best moments of TV shows or movies are not always the best dialogue, but the best visual moments—what was the most GIFable?

I needed a gimmick. Something cute, playful, something fun and current. Something Tumblr would eat up. I got out my computer and scrolled through the One Direction tag and saw a fan edit that was adorable. It was of the boys onstage, with photoshopped flower crowns atop their heads. This trend was sweeping tween fashion, filtering all the way to fan edits of boy bands. Then it hit me. Why not give people the real version of what they'd been spending so much time using Photoshop to create?

Now, this plan had a few holes in it. Number one, I didn't have any flower crowns, nor did I know where I could buy them with a day's notice. How do you search "hippie shit" on Yelp?! Number two, I didn't know if they'd go along with it. At press junkets, talent sits in a room full of lights and cameras, and different publications cycle in and out with about four minutes of face time each. From the second you enter the room, your timer starts, and you have to get down to business. If I suggested they put on flower crowns and they didn't like it, it not only wasted time that could have been spent interviewing, but it also sets the mood for an awkward interview. This was a huge risk. I had to make this work.

The next day, I woke up early and called my good friend Alex and asked him if he wanted to tag along for the secret adventure. Like the angel he is, he dropped everything and joined me on my quest for flower crowns. We searched endless boutiques and chain stores, finding nothing like what I envisioned. It was time to get crafty. I bought a handful of flowerless-vine crowns at one boutique and as many flower hair clips from Forever 21 as I could and began to Martha Stewart that shit together with a hot glue gun. They were perfect. I was ready, with less than an hour to spare. It was time.

We arrived back at the hotel to hundreds of teenage girls lining the street, screaming at our arrival. We checked in, made our way upstairs to the press waiting room, and sat among adults with BlackBerrys. In my DIY flower crown and lilac hair, I definitely felt out of place. I checked my Twitter and saw that the buzz had spread about my arrival, and I suddenly felt the weight of the interview on my shoulders. This wasn't just about making a fun interview for my channel, it was also about asking the boys questions that the fandom wanted asked. I was representing, to a degree, people who spent every day hoping for a favorite or a follow. I took a look at my note cards, got out my pen, trusted my gut, and crossed out the safe questions I had prepared. I wrote down the real questions I would want to hear answered.

"Tyler?" a voice said from the hallway.

It was time.

I made my way down the hall, into an elevator, down another hall, and took a seat. I could hear muffled voices in the hotel room I was waiting outside of, followed by the unmistakable sound of Niall laughing. This was happening. I reviewed my last-minute changes on my note cards, wiped my sweaty palms on my jeans, and reminded myself to smile and have fun. As the previous interviewer made her way out of the room, I clutched five flower crowns, adjusted my own, stood up, rounded the corner, and entered the room.

What you typically see in an interview is a tight shot of celebrities in front of a backdrop. What I saw was the truth of the grand production: cords running every which way, bright boxlights illuminating faces and softening imperfections, and people—so many people, from producers, management, sound teams, and publicists to handlers, makeup artists, stylists, and marketers. The production behind this day was intense. I ducked as I swooped into the set, stepping in toward the five boys, who were chatting among themselves about the previous interview.

As the producer announced my arrival, I shook hands with the boys one by one and introduced myself.

Niall's eyes lit up, "This guy's very famous."

My heart stopped.

"I see you all over Twitter . . . ," Harry added.

I was officially dead.

Before I realized it, the cameras were rolling, and it was time to get my fucking shit together and make them put on these damn flower crowns. I would *not* be the only one sporting a casual tween floral look in this room.

If you want to see the video, go to my YouTube channel and check out "Tyler Oakley Interviews One Direction."

It's exciting to build up the hype of a huge video, but it's even more exciting to drop a bomb out of the blue, Beyoncé-style. I've done it for a few special events, such as when I interviewed Michelle Obama, but nothing will match the explosion that occurred on August 30, 2013, when I uploaded my video interviewing One Direction. Pandemonium in the YouTube fandom, insanity in the One Direction fandom; it was madness.

From then on, One Direction became so much a part of my online presence that I rarely went a day without tweeting to or about them. I completely submerged myself into their community and immediately became a fixture there. A couple months later, I was offered the chance to interview the boys once again on the day of their album launch, during their twenty-four-hour livestream aptly named 1D Day. Hundreds of thousands of teens all over the world would be watching—this was an opportunity like no other. Not only did I get to play a game with Zayn and Louis wherein Zayn joked that his middle name was Beyoncé (which later became an inside joke for the fandom), but I also got to hang out behind the cameras with Niall. It all culminated with me onstage participating in a live sing-along of "White Christmas" with the boys, Jerry Springer, and Michael Bublé. Weird day.

And just as fast as it went up, it all came crumbling down.

Some people spend the majority of their online lives tweeting their favorite celebrities hoping that one day, maybe, a celebrity might favorite their tweet and acknowledge their existence. Rarely will you get a reply. On January 19, my 11:11 wishes came true—but I should have been more careful of what I wished for.

Basically, a member of One Direction tweeted his support of the family values of a TV personality who had recently come under fire for homophobic remarks he made in a magazine profile. I tweeted expressing concern and hoping for clarity. The band member then tweeted directly at me saying I was never a fan. And then, shit hit the fan.

When I first saw his reply, my stomach dropped and my

heart began to race. I quickly turned on Skype and called my friend and fellow YouTuber Troye Sivan to ask him what to do. Nobody else knew the complexities of fandom and the Internet like Troye, and together we weighed the options. Within minutes, #WeWantTylerOakleyDead began trending worldwide. It was as if I went from the fandom's favorite supporter to their most despised traitor, and there was no going back.

I felt hurt and betrayed. I had spent years publicly supporting this band, dedicating so much of my online presence to them, and it all went down the drain because a member of the band decided to very publicly throw a fit. In that moment, I was sure that my online identity was ruined, my career as a YouTuber was over, and my relationship with my audience was tainted. Texts from YouTubers flooded in acknowledging how much my situation sucked, and my mom even called to make sure I was safe. I was mad and disappointed and sad and sick to my stomach, with no clue what to do.

I knew that if I continued the Twitter banter, it would only get worse. I thanked him for clearing up the confusion, acknowledged the death threats that were riddling my feed, and announced I'd be stepping away from the Internet for a minute to regroup. I went to bed that night questioning what it would be like to wake up the next day afraid of the Internet for the first time in my life.

When I woke up, it was still terrible. The fandom found reimaginations of their first hashtag, such as #LiamSlayedTyler, #RIPTylerOakleysCareer, and #WeHateYouTyler, all trending worldwide throughout the next day. Over the following week, I decided to shut my laptop and contemplate what I had done. I reexamined my words, actions, and questioned if I had overstepped or spoken irrationally. What I found was that after every reconsideration, I still stood by what I had said. I held someone that I respected accountable for his actions—plain and simple. It was something that I would hope my own followers would do if I ever said something that alienated them. The misunderstanding itself was not what was disappointing; but how he handled the incident hurt, not to mention the sheeplike mentality of his fans. These things had nothing to do with me.

So I let it go. After my week of impromptu vacation, I felt ready to return. I decided to come back not with spite or anger, but with a call to action for my own people. I asked them to be inclusive, to hold me accountable for my actions, and to support each other and make our family a positive environment. My return was poignant and the tiniest bit cheeky, but it set the foundation for the expectations I've had ever since.

Almost two years later, I feel free—as silly as it sounds. What sometimes felt like a topic I always had to mention or talk about now is something I have regained control over. Throughout my now eight years online, I've found that what I want to give to the world is my decision. As soon as I feel bound by expectations, it's okay to step back, reevaluate whether it's actually something that I want to give, and proceed accordingly.

I've moved on from the "1D professional fangirl" era of my online life, though I still remain a fan of the music—and it seems the boys have grown a bit too. As of the week I'm writing this, Zayn has officially left the band. Sometimes doing what's right for your conscience is not always the most popular decision, but I can guarantee that in retrospect you won't regret the choice you made.

what michelle obama smells like

ONE OF THE STRANGEST QUESTIONS I GET about celebrities that I've met is "What do they smell like?" When did this become a thing? When asked about Harry Styles, I typically say he smells like sunshine and happiness, because obviously he does. But who really takes a whiff of a celebrity when so much more important things have to be considered during a brief encounter?

For example, I'm more interested in asking Gaga what *really* happened at her "Edge of Glory" music-video shoot than sniffing her. Is that wrong? Do I have misguided priorities?

When I met Michelle Obama, yes, obviously viewers cared about what we discussed, but also at the top of their resounding, must-know concerns was her scent. What are they expecting me to say? That she stank? That she was so rancid that I had to hold my breath as we did the double-cheek kiss? That she was so pungent that I questioned the health of her dogs Sunny and Bo? Okay, well, I'm here to finally answer the question of what Michelle Obama smelled like, and it's not what you'd expect.

When I first got the e-mail from the White House asking if I'd be interested in collaborating with Michelle Obama, I immediately got on Twitter and frantically made sure I've never made a joke about Queen Michelle. I've always loved her, but I have a bad habit of poking fun at those I love. If I was actually going to be in the presence of her incredibly muscled arms, I needed to delete all evidence of such. Finding nothing but praise and adoration, I replied with one of the easiest *Duhs* I've ever sent. Yes, the White House and I are that casual. Probably because just seven months earlier, I was lucky enough to have had a meeting with President Barack Obama.*

Michelle was on a publicity campaign for Reach Higher, which encouraged students to attend college after graduating from high school. As a first-generation college-goer, I was a great fit for the campaign, so I submitted my questions to the White House team for approval. She would be doing two interviews, the first with Sway at MTV, a legendary staple of the iconic station, someone whom I've watched for over a decade. The other? Some blue-haired twink from the Internet. (Me.)

My first request was that the interview be dropped on my channel like a Beyoncé album—with no hype, just a quiet demonstration of who's the boss of YouTube, at the click of a button. Approved. Then we discussed creative logistics. On my

---

* A handful of other YouTube creators and I met with the president in the Roosevelt Room, where we discussed the power of youth on the Internet. Afterward, he gave us a tour of his office. All the other YouTubers around me were making great impressions, and I felt I had to say something. I blurted out, "Cute desk." To the president. Of the United States.

YouTube channel, I often do a two-part collaboration style with traditional celebrities. The first part is an interview-like portion that allows them to discuss the talking points their publicists insist upon. The second part consists of taking turns to see how many questions each person can answer in one minute. These questions are written on little strips of paper that are pulled out of a hat.

"What type of hat will it be?" asked the White House representative. Every little detail needed to be preauthorized, including the hat. I explained to the official that I would be bringing the cutest, little summery hat that was a subtle banana-crème yellow and was adorable with navy short shorts. With zero amusement, they said okay, implying that the full, exact description would go through the approval process. Let's hope this administration loves pastels.

Apparently, they did. My concept was approved, and I would have about twenty minutes with the first lady to film. I was to fly out secretly the next night, immediately following the 2014 Streamy Awards. I was nominated for Streamy Entertainer of the Year, the final award of the evening, so I had to stay until the very end. Regardless of the outcome, I'd book it directly from the Streamys to the airport and hopefully not miss my flight. Either I'd be carrying an award right offstage and directly into my car, or I'd quietly be slipping out the back, empty-handed (but still winning, because I had a playdate with Michelle Obama the next day).

Luckily, thanks to my people (read: you), the votes poured in, and I was on top! I went up to accept my award, and I talked about all the amazing opportunities YouTube had brought me.

In the back of my mind, I was thinking about the opportunity of a lifetime scheduled for the following day, but about which nobody in the room had any clue.

I hopped offstage and weaved through the crowd toward the exit. In the backseat of the car, my friend Korey and I changed from our black-tie attire into our airplane sweats. We made it to the terminal on time, boarded our flight, and reclined our seats to sleep on the red-eye to Atlanta. I tried my darnedest to sleep, but this was a career-defining interview, and it felt like the night before Christmas. I couldn't believe that one of the most powerful women in the world found value in me, my career, and the positive impact the Internet can make. Meanwhile, in the hold of the plane, my suitcase was shifting—quietly crushing my cute, summery, subtle-banana-crème-yellow hat. I had no clue.

We landed in Atlanta, where Michelle was to have a pep rally at a local high school, and we made our way to our hotel to shower and get ready. With a thud, I hoisted my suitcase onto my hotel-room bed. Piece by piece, I took out my clothes to be ironed and readied. At the bottom of my bag, underneath a pair of dress shoes, I spotted a subtle-banana-crème color peeking through. Oh, no. I yanked out my cutest, little summery hat, but it was too late. Devastated, I held the crinkled hat in my hands, like a family pet that had been hit by a car.

"This simply won't do," I sighed dramatically (as usual).

Korey rolled his eyes. "Okay, we'll find something else to put the questions in." He searched the sparse hotel room for something—*anything*—that was at once classy, playful, stylish, functional, seasonal, effortless, and yet plain enough to be appropriate for the task. We found a silver ice bucket—chic yet ordinary. This was the best and only option. I put it in my book bag, and we made our way downstairs. One little wrench in the works was not going to ruin my most important collaboration ever!

En route to the high school, I reviewed the questions with Korey and did final preparations for the video. I was prepared— maybe overprepared—and I couldn't wait. We got to the school and went through security without a hitch. We were led to the gym, where we waited among the government suits with their BlackBerrys, on the side of an elevated platform. The room was full of eager teens rambunctiously cheering in anticipation of the Queen. Without warning, she arrived, making her way onto the stage with a casual elegance and immediately captivating the room.

She delivered her speech to roaring applause, pausing only to call over paramedics because a teen in the front row fainted halfway through. Presumably this was due to locked knees and lack of fresh air, but honestly, I was like *Yes kid I feel you look at her arms they are more astounding than they are in the magazines I'm about to faint too!*

At the end of her plea for higher education, she stepped down, smiling and waving until she disappeared backstage. "You ready?" a White House Official whispered in my direction, eyes never leaving his BlackBerry. I was as ready as I'd ever be.

We were escorted to the school's library, where MTV had set up an area with two chairs, proper lighting, and campaign branding. I was taken into a conference room adjacent to the shelves of books, and I began to situate my things.

"Ummmmmmmmmmmmmmmm."

I looked up at the White House Official. His eyes had left his BlackBerry and were now fixed on the ice bucket in my hand. Given the reaction I was seeing in his eyes, I looked down to confirm that I was in fact holding a bucket and not a hand grenade.

"Oh, uhhh, my cute hat was kinda beat-up from being in my luggage on the flight, so I brought this instead." He turned, raised his hand to his earpiece, and whispered with great urgency, "There is no hat. There is an ice bucket." After a moment, he dropped his hand, turned, and left the room without a word.

I sat in silence, already mic'ed and too paranoid to voice my concerns out loud. I looked at Korey with a Literally, what the fuck was that? face, to which his expression seemed to reply, I have no clue what the fuck is happening right now. Minutes passed, and I could definitely feel my armpits getting nice and damp and unacceptable for the presence of Queen Michelle.

The White House Official made his way back into the room and with a hard stare delivered the news. "An ice bucket sends a message of support for the alcohol industry, which is not aligned messaging with the first lady's campaign."

"Ummmmmmmmmmmmmmmmm"—my eyes darted around the room—"let me see if I can find something else to use then?"

The White House Official put his hand to his ear again; he turned his head slightly, listening. After a moment he announced, "You have three minutes."

With that, Korey and I went to work. We burst out of the conference room and back into the main library, looking for something—anything—that communicated a PG-rated, campaign-aligned message of going to college, without the highly frowned-upon message of blacking out while there. My eyes scanned back and forth, searching, until they fell on the front desk of the library. There, among card catalogs and hand sanitizer, was a wicker basket filled with apples. With no time to spare, I dumped the apples all over the desk, some rolling onto the floor as I spun around, wicker in hand, and power walked back to the White House Official—all with the determination of a nine-year-old scavenger-hunt winner.

As I approached, his hand went to the earpiece. "The ice bucket has been replaced with a wicker basket." A moment went by that felt like an eternity. His eyes met mine. "You're approved."

My sigh of relief coincided with a quiet gasp from the room, as Michelle made her way through the front door.

She greeted us with hugs, handshakes, and warm smiles. The mood of the room lightened instantly, and we positioned ourselves for the interview. The White House Official, obviously sensing that things were going according to plan, leaned over to me and whispered, "Due to timing, we no longer have twenty minutes. You'll have seven minutes to conduct the interview." I looked at him with eyes that said, *How dare you right now*, but a smile that said, *That's perfect, I'm a professional who only needs one take.* His reply was to tap his phone, indicating he had started the timer.

The interview portion went swimmingly: laughs were had, I called her "my queen" on camera—she exceeded my every expectation and was one of the most playful and ideal interviews

I had ever conducted. With the timer ticking, I reached down to pull the question-filled wicker basket onto my lap, while simultaneously introducing the second segment.

"Ohhh! Nice wicker basket!"

I couldn't tell if the compliment was real. Had the basket been approved based on White House knowledge of the first lady's passion for wicker? Or was she mocking me and imagining the hilarity of my flying across the country with this ludicrous object as my carry-on? Either way, it was approved, and this segment was *happening*. She casually answered my quirky questions, indicating zero knowledge of the drama behind the basket at hand. With the interview compete and a minute left on the clock, the first lady and I hugged. Over her shoulder, I locked eyes with the White House Official and smiled. When life throws a wrench in your plans, catch it and build an IKEA bookshelf—or in this case, an incredible collaboration.

The first lady has many passions and concerns for the world. While this campaign was about higher education, she also uses her influence to raise awareness of childhood obesity, with healthy eating being a staple of her messaging. Although I look back at our brief encounter fondly, when I'm asked what Michelle Obama smells like, I can't help but recall the haunting scent of hastily discarded, bruised apples. Most likely, these were the only healthy foods ever disrespected in her name, and she had absolutely no way of knowing. Until now.

how fitting

ONE OF THE WEIRD, HOLLYWOOD-TYPE THINGS I have somehow been allowed to do is to host and report from red-carpet events. Back when I was in Michigan, the closest I ever got to the glitz and glamour of LA was my Hollywood-themed prom. A step and repeat was at the entrance, and volunteer parents lined up outside the gym to act like paparazzi. Somehow, this was only slightly less fake than life in LA.

Now that I live in Hollywood, I sometimes get invited to play the showbiz game, including red carpets, TV appearances, and award shows. When you watch these things from home, they flow seamlessly. It's as if self-congratulating ceremonies with celebrities patting each other on the back are second nature to the Hollywood elite. But don't be fooled! A lot of work goes into these things. Typically, this is a full-scale production, with stylists and makeup teams and hair people all primping and grooming their subjects. The number of man-hours that go into forty seconds on a red carpet would blow any Midwesterner's mind.

When I first started getting invites to events, I'd show up and feel so inappropriately dressed and out of place. It was like I wasn't even the same species as these people. I'd be surrounded by celebrities, each being lint-rolled and straightened and adjusted and perfected by stylists, while I stood in an ill-fitting suit, plucking off my own lint like a shunned chimp. Celebrities stood tall, smoldering into the camera. My posture looked Neanderthal, and my expression looked as though a human child had just taught me what smiling is. I'd then move to my spot on the press line, where I'd attempt to string together sentences that made vague sense, as sweat dripped down my protruding brow. Celebrities looked at me like I was an intern or a contest winner at best—at worst, I was a crazy Twitter fan that had photoshopped and laminated a press pass.

Luckily, these A-listers had mercy on my poor soul, and they approached my interviews with patience. Over time, I've kind of grown out of my awkwardness, and now I'm able to act like a human on red carpets. In my time spent interviewing celebrities, I mainly struggle with the temptation to ask them to follow me on Twitter.

Over the years, I've collected a few highlights on red carpets, typically from the most unlikely interviews. Yeardley Smith, the voice of Lisa Simpson, used her interview with me to promote her line of purple suede pumps. I basked in her glory and let her self-promote shamelessly. Julie Bowen, best known as Claire Dunphy on the sitcom *Modern Family*, asked me during an interview how I was allowed to be up past my bedtime. It was 5:00 p.m. on a Sunday. I once told Paris Hilton that her song "Stars Are Blind" changed the music game and was an anthem for true music lovers. I've discussed butts with the boys of 5 Seconds of Summer, and I used my interview with Nicki Minaj to thank her for retweeting me, six years after the fact.

When I approach red carpets, I always think of what Oprah recalls as the single most important lesson she's learned while doing television: we all want to be validated. Oprah said that after almost every single interview (of the thirty-five thousand she's done in her career), the interviewee turns to Oprah and asks, "Was that okay?" Knowing this, I try to remember that everyone is just trying their best, me included. Sure, some people are better known than others, but that's not a reason to be intimidated by them. If anything, I've found that the more famous someone is, the more they just want to be seen by one person, in one moment, and to have some spontaneous fun, for once, in their overly regimented day. As I've worked more and more carpets, I've tried to just enjoy it. You can study all you want, and you can prepare certain questions for certain attendees, but once the carpet starts, you have no clue what is going to happen—except that people will show up and want to be seen, heard, and understood. In the monotony of the same questions over and over, they'll hope for a few fun ones. My goal is to see them, hear them, and to goof around for a few minutes.

After a few years of working the carpets for the MTV VMAs, Kids' Choice Awards, the MTV Movie Awards, and various TrevorLIVEs, I started to see more and more opportunities come to me. In 2015, I got my first offer to work the red carpet of the *Grammys*, and I was thrilled. For previous red-carpet gigs, I had always simply gotten dressed the morning of wondering, *Okay, what's going to make me look minimally lumpy today?* As someone who has been on the Worst Dressed List and described as "Caesar Flickerman's bastard son," I've developed a sense for what fashion critics are looking to eviscerate. For the Grammys, I needed to look good. I wanted something tasteful but fun, classic but edgy, colorful but understated—so I hired a stylist.

After a couple fittings in which I picked out some favorite suits, I decided to borrow an olive-green Armani suit with a navy shirt and pocket square and a silver-striped tie. The morning I arrived to work the Grammys, my stylist was there to help me put on the finishing touches, and I felt incredible. The suit was tailored for my exact measurements, and I felt that I finally belonged among the red-carpet tribe.

After a full day of promo shoots, interviews, and walking the carpet myself, the team cheered as we called it a wrap. Though I loved my suit, nothing beats a pair of sweatpants. I shed my Armani and opted for pajamas for the ride home.

With a paper bag full of the day's borrowed outfit between my legs in the backseat of the car, I sighed and smiled, savoring the success of the day. I closed my eyes and daydreamed. Maybe someday I'll have a stylist for every event, or even better, one for my own talk show. I imagined custom-made suits to make me feel comfortable for every night in front of the camera. Someday. My driver slowed to a stop, and I opened my eyes. I grabbed my Armani-filled grocery bag, and I stepped out of the car and into my apartment. Completely exhausted, I dropped my things at the entrance and called it a night.

The next morning, I woke up to the sound of my 6:00 a.m. alarm, and I groaned while crawling out of bed. I had to be on the NBC lot for a 7:00 a.m. call for an *Access Hollywood* shoot, recapping the Grammys. Normally, it takes me thirty minutes to even get out of bed, but somehow I was up, showered, dressed in a fresh suit, and ready to go—all way ahead of schedule. I decided to use the extra time to clean my apartment. I did some dishes, put away some laundry, and emptied all my garbage cans. Deciding to take all three bags out in one trip, I struggled through the back door and threw them into my empty Dumpster. As I got into my car, I saw a homeless man rifling through my neighbor's trash, with a grocery cart full of cans beside him. While many of my non-LA friends were typically mortified by this sight, I've gotten pretty used to it, unfortunately. LA has a huge homeless population, and you'll often see many of them going through recycling bins for cans and bottles to return for cash.

I got into my car, made my way to the NBC lot, filmed my segment, and headed back home. During my drive, I got a call from my buddy Korey, who had just received word from my stylist that the Armani suit had to be returned that day. Unsure if I'd be home when they planned to pick it up, I asked Korey to head over to my place.

After twenty minutes, I got a second call from Korey. "Where did you say the suit was?"

"In a paper bag somewhere? Maybe near the front door?" I was focused on the road.

"I looked everywhere. There aren't any paper bags anywhere."

My stomach dropped. In my hurry that morning, while cleaning my apartment . . . no. I couldn't have. In complete disbelief, I involuntarily burst out laughing.

"What?"

"I think"—I began, in between gasps of laughter—"I think I threw it away?" I screamed hysterically while cackling, *"Korey! I totally threw it away! Oh my God, I am five minutes away. I will meet you at my back door. Be ready to hoist me into the Dumpster."*

After I parked, I scurried to my back door, where I found Korey peeking into the Dumpster. I laughed maniacally as I approached, still shaking my head at how clueless I was.

He cringed as I got to him. "I don't think it's in there."

I brushed by him and opened the top of the Dumpster to peer inside. Sure enough, it was completely empty, just like this morning, except for two of the three garbage bags I had thrown inside hours earlier. Missing was the third and final paper bag. I knew what had happened to it. Somewhere in West Hollywood, a homeless man was collecting cans and bottles from recycling bins, clad head to toe in custom-fitted Armani (just not custom-fitted for *him*). I called my stylist to let her know what had happened, positive that this was by far the worst first impression I could ever make with anyone.

Now, every time I throw garbage into that Dumpster, I can't help but double-check to make sure it's not a $3,000 suit. I like to imagine that someday, ten years from now, when I'm on my way to my job as a late-night-talk-show host, I'll be stopped at a red light. I'll look over to the people at the bus stop, and he'll be there, a tall, lanky homeless man in an olive-green Armani suit, fully tailored to a size completely unlike his own.

Side note: A few months later, on my twenty-sixth-birthday weekend, I developed a stomach flu. It was terrible timing. I had to cancel going to an award show, postpone my birthday plans, and cancel a trip to Hawaii. As part of this glorious weekend on the toilet, I had to return a stool sample to my doctor, so he could make sure no small creature was living inside my stomach. In my dizzy, dehydrated frenzy to get out of the house after three days of terrible diarrhea to take my shit to the doctor, I also grabbed some of the garbage that had been piling up at my front door. I tossed it all in the Dumpster and took three steps before stopping in my tracks, realizing that I had tossed it *all* in— shit included. I needed that shit. That shit was important. My doctor specially requested it. After months of diligently making sure that nothing I threw into the Dumpster was anything more valuable than actual human feces, I had accidentally thrown my actual human feces into the Dumpster. I couldn't go to the doctor without it, so I pitifully hoisted my frail body in to pull it out. On your twenty-sixth birthday, nothing says adulthood more than fishing your own shit out of a Dumpster.

ten cummandments

SAN FRANCISCO TAUGHT ME A LOT OF THINGS. For example, some people have the innate ability to wink at you, while walking in your direction, while peeing! Also, if you live in the Castro, you can sometimes go weeks without seeing straight people and forget they even exist! But my favorite lessons of all had to do with sex. In such a sinner's town, it's curious to think that with what I learned, I could write a Bible of teachings. So, without further ado, please enjoy . . .

The Ten Cummandments I Learned While Living in the Bay Area

THOU SHALT NOT FANG BANG

In a town where everyone lets their freak flag fly, I guess I shouldn't be surprised when I meet people who are unashamed to announce their fetishes early on in a relationship. This is, of course, a town that hosts festivals like the Folsom Street Fair—an outdoors celebration of all things BDSM, where leather is mandatory, and I once saw a woman willingly getting her "downstairs" whipped. These things happen in broad daylight in the streets of San Francisco, so what did I expect of the gentlemen I met in the shadows of the city's gay bars?

One of these fellows showed no out-of-the-box quirks at the bar, and he was kind enough to let me crash at his place. This is where I quickly learned the level of drunk I needed to be to ignore weird things during sex—meaning, I was *way* too sober to be hooking up with a guy wearing fangs. No, they weren't the plastic, glow-in-the-dark ones you get out of a gumball machine—these were the real deal. Okay, not real as in attached to an undead Transylvanian aristocrat—they were just expensive-looking veneers. This was not my cup of tea, but at least this man respected his kink enough to go first-class all the way. Listen, when it's 2:30 a.m., desperate times call for desperate measures, so you've gotta let Count Fuckula drain you dry. (No twinks were harmed during the learning of this cummandment.)

THOU SHALT TAME THY MANE

Some people are hairy. I can appreciate this, but everyone has his limits. During my San Francisco days, a guy spent the night. The morning after, he sat up against my headboard, arms spread, inviting me to come cuddle into him. Half-asleep and without my glasses, I moved into his embrace, until I felt like I was being smothered by some type of musky wig.

Bewildered and mortified, I rolled away on the bed to grab my glasses, and I looked back to find him smiling, sitting upright, hands behind his head. His overgrown armpit bushes were a visual assault, like a glob of spit or a booger, I couldn't look away. I didn't know what to say or do. So I just sat and fumbled on my phone and waited to see how long he'd sit like that. Eventually, he took one hand and slowly lifted it toward the opposite armpit, where—no exaggeration—he began to *run his fingers through it*. Every man has his limit, and apparently mine was his finger-combing his Rapunzel-esque armpit locks.

THOU SHALT NOT STEAL

After one particular adult slumber party, I awoke to find my new friend hopping into his jeans, trying to make as little sound as possible.

"Leaving so soon?"

"Yeah, I've got a brunch to get to. . . . Don't worry about me, go back to bed," he whispered as he leaned over to kiss me. I stretched and snuggled into my pillow, closing my eyes and whispering good-bye to him.

About an hour later, I woke up again to the sound of my roommate, Korey, yelling from downstairs, *"Did you use my hair stuff?"* I heard his footsteps coming up my stairs, and he tapped on my door. "Where's my hair stuff?" He peeked through the crack of my door.

"I don't know . . . just use mine."

He returned downstairs and a moment later yelled up again. *"Yours is gone too!"*

My eyes shot open, in shock and disbelief. I leaped out of bed and flew downstairs to see what else might be missing. That motherfucker had come over, slept in my bed, cuddled with me all night, and left with *my hair products*. This is why we can't have nice things.

Just as Korey had said, our bathroom cabinet was completely empty, with all styling pastes, waxes, and hair sprays missing. Yet, nothing else seemed to be gone. Even my laptop lay untouched, out in the open, right next to the front door. Our thief had no desire for expensive technology—no, this sicko craved something specific: a perfect and effortless quiff. I may not remember his face, but I *will* recognize his hair, and when I do . . . revenge will be mine.

THOU SHALT BE THIS TALL TO RIDE THIS RIDE

It's no secret that I dig shorter guys. Or, if it was, *now you know*. This is not to say I won't also date and/or love taller guys. Times are tough, and beggars can't be choosers.

I met one short guy while I was getting pizza one night at 2:00 a.m. He was probably five feet two, with a compact build and a charming smile. After a bit of conversation, I found out he used to be in the army—I was into it.

He spent the night, and after he left in the morning, my roommate, Korey, appeared, determined to get the gossip on the night before. While we chatted, Korey noticed a step stool in front of my window, awkwardly out of place. We both looked at it, then at each other, curiously.

"Why is that there?" he asked.

"I . . . have no idea."

We sat for a second before it hit Korey: *"He was too short to reach up and close the blinds!"*

Korey burst out laughing. I screamed and clasped my hands over my mouth, trying not to wake the neighbors.

THOU SHALT NOT LEAVE YOUR FAVORITE SWEAT-PANTS BEHIND

No matter how much you like a guy, you *never* know when things may turn sour. With this in mind, it's imperative to keep all of your beloved items in your own possession, even if things seem to be going well at the time. I once dated a boy in San Francisco, and I left my favorite pair of Okemos High School wrestling-team sweatpants at his apartment. After a long weekend out of town and a few curt texts back and forth, I quickly realized I was probably not going to be seeing him anymore. Worse, I wouldn't be seeing my favorite piece of athletic apparel ever again. Don't repeat my mistake.

THOU SHALT AVOID TRAINERS

I once developed a weird cuddle relationship with a guy I met through a dating app. He was conventionally handsome, a personal trainer with a body that was borderline upsetting, and the perfect big spoon. We made a habit of hanging out and watching a movie, after which he'd log on to his IMDb account and give it 8 stars. It didn't matter if Meryl Streep gave her all-time best performance, or if it was *Fifty Shades of Grey*. We'd then fall asleep spooning. Nothing sexy, just some good old-fashioned half-asleep grinding. This happened a few times, right up until I finally encountered his true, weird colors.

As we were trying to figure out what movie to watch, he took a sip of his drink and asked if I wanted anything.

"That lemonade looks good, thanks."

"Hmmm, I don't think I have any lemonade." He walked to the fridge.

I looked at him, trying to read if he was joking. Straight-faced and clueless, he took a sip of his drink, a murky, whitish, thick liquid that I had spent all night assuming was lemonade.

I felt uneasy. "Wait . . . what are you drinking then?"

He smiled and pulled a carton of egg whites out of his fridge. I squinted to make sure my eyes weren't deceiving me as he topped off his glass.

"No . . ." My jaw dropped as he gulped half of his glass down.

"Good for personal training!" He put the carton back in the fridge. He came back to his bed, pressed play on the movie, assumed his position behind me as my big-spoon cuddle buddy, and treated me to the most distinct egg breath I'd ever experienced. I could have sworn he was deliberately breathing extrahard behind me, and my stomach felt wobbly for the rest of the night.

THOU SHALT NOT FANGIRL

There's nothing wrong with knowing a bit of background about the person you're about to hook up with. In fact, I encourage it. Nowadays, with the Internet at your fingertips, you should utilize this resource not only to find new potential partners, but also to make sure they aren't serial killers.

This does pose a problem when your entire existence is online. I like to keep it casual, like when people ask me what I do, I'll say something like "Brand marketing" and withhold that I am the brand and my Twitter is the marketing. Of course, some guys already know the scoop about me. Sometimes they're casual, and sometimes they're not. Sometimes they act like they have no clue who I am when in fact they've seen every video. One guy, after we hooked up, asked for a selfie.

THOU SHALT KNOW WHO YOU'RE FUCKIN'

One of my favorite getaway weekends during my time in San Francisco was to Lake Tahoe. Fifteen of my SF gays and I made the journey all the way to a huge log cabin, complete with plenty of bunk beds, a hot tub, and a five-minute walk to the beach. Most of our time at the cabin was spent drinking, and one night everyone decided it was a good time to get outrageously drunk.

My friend Lucas was an especially slop mess that night, which was pretty normal for him, but when Lucas was drunk, Lucas went on the prowl. We soon realized his goal was Jason, another guy in our group, who looked a bit like me. The rest of us whispered among ourselves, as we knew those two were going to end up fucking. We gave them their privacy as they made their way to the six-bunk communal bedroom. As I snuck through to grab my toothbrush before bed, sure enough, they were at it, loud and unashamed. Good for them!

The next morning, as I scrubbed dishes in the kitchen, I heard someone coming up the stairs: slop-mess Lucas.

He was wide-awake and groaning from his hangover. "So about last night . . ."

"Oh, girl, y'all were *gone*."

"Yeah, I just don't want the rest of the trip to be weird between the two of us." He began to massage my shoulders.

I put down the dish I was scrubbing, turned around, and

looked at him, puzzled. "Wait. What are you talking about?" I couldn't believe what I thought was happening.

"It's no biggie! We're friends, and friends have fun sometimes." He went in for a hug.

"Lucas! That was Jason you were fucking! Not me!" I screamed, before letting out a witchlike cackle.

I spent the rest of the weekend screaming at Lucas between fits of uncontrollable laughter. Get drunk and have fun, but, girl, don't get so drunk you don't know *who* you're having fun with.

THOU SHALT NOT CATFISH

Catfishing is when you lie about your identity to someone else online. The term is relatively new, originating from a documentary starring Nev Schulman, where (spoiler alert) he gets catfished. Nev then created a TV show where he helps people who think they're getting catfished meet the people they're talking to online. It's horrifying. We'll get to that show later.

I was introduced to catfishing early on because my Grandma Oakley was the victim of a catfish.

Grandma Oakley was what you might call an early adopter of the Internet. If you tried to call her, you'd get a busy signal, as she'd more often than not be online with her dial-up Internet, in chat rooms. She was always talking to someone. We didn't find out who until about a decade later.

Before I get to that, let me explain Grandma Oakley. For decades, she worked at the local grocery store—Meijer— where she bagged groceries 365 days a year. She was in a bowling league, and after their games they'd have block parties and she'd get so drunk that she'd have to be taken home in a wheelbarrow. While I was growing up, Grandma Oakley lived in a trailer park, with my uncle and cousin, and her poodle named Peanut. She'd often babysit me, and the only game she had on Nintendo was a casino game. My grandpa died before I was born, and I always knew my Grandma Oakley to be single—or so I thought.

Not until recently did my family find out that for all those years my grandma was romantically involved with a stranger online. He claimed to be a younger NASCAR driver who also worked at the Vatican. Either Grandma Oakley had found her ideal match, or she was getting catfished. I might have bad news for you, Grandma.

Shocked, appalled, and fascinated by the phenomenon of catfishing, I was ready to embark on a catfish journey myself. MTV (casual name-drop) called to ask if I wanted to cohost an episode of their show *Catfish*, and I went along for the ride. Knowing how unrealistic and scripted the majority of "reality" television is, I had low hopes. But after a week on the road with the production, I can safely say that *catfishers exist*. People do lie about who they are, and people put up with years of lying. In that one week, I pursed my lips, widened my eyes, and shook my head in disbelief more than ever before in my life.

At the end of my episode, it was revealed that (spoiler!) the two people involved were actually who they said they were. The person was *not* being catfished, but was just talking to someone who didn't want to meet in person. Yikes.

When all was said and done, I realized the scariest form

of catfishing: when people are honest about what they look like or what their job is, but not about who they are as a person. You can easily spot through your peephole whether someone looks like the pictures he sent you, but can you also detect rudeness, selfishness, or, even worse, if they don't appreciate *The Golden Girls* or ranch dressing?

It doesn't matter if someone really is a NASCAR driver or really does look like a GQ model if at the end of the day he is horrible to be around. Over time, people's true colors show. They may have told you that they enjoy museums while you were talking on Tinder, but often enough they just wanted to seem cultured. They actually spend their Saturdays watching *Judge Judy* marathons (which might be preferable). Listen! My grandma thought she was going to fall in love with the pope's right-hand man, and look where that got her! *How am I supposed to believe in love?!*

No, no, no . . . not all those you meet online are lying about who they are or what they're into. In fact, I once chatted with someone online who was 100 percent himself in every way, from his profile picture to his very, very specific interests. We'll call that cummandment "Thou Shall Embrace Thy Fetish"—and that one gets its own chapter, coming next.

hopeless toemantic

A few cardinal rules to being stereotypically gay are:

1. No carpenter jeans.

2. Overuse the painting-nails emoji while texting.

3. Have an overly self-conscious Grindr profile.

If you're unfamiliar with Grindr, let me break it down for you. It's an app that lets you see who the closest gays are, as well as how far away they are from your location. It's perfect for stalking hot bearded guys, if you're into that, which I am. Your Grindr profile is a quick snapshot into who you are as a gay—it includes your interests, your general background, and what you're looking for in a partner. Some gays spend years perfecting their profiles, trying to put forward their most message-worthy selves—attempting to find (some level of) love in a (relatively) hopeless place.

Depending on where you are in the world, the location-based, person-to-person app can work wonders. For example, I grew up in Michigan, where so few gays were logged in that the closest ones often included people in Ohio at Cedar Point. At the other end of the spectrum, during my time in San Francisco, the closest user could be as close as three feet away from you, which was often an overestimate due to GPS accuracy errors.

Now, I know some of you ladies at home may be thinking, "Wow, I love gays, I'm looking for a gay best friend, this is the perfect networking app for me!" *No. Stop it.* We are not collectibles, and considering the nonpremium version only shows the two hundred closest people, your being in our feed could bump our soul mate out of the queue, so don't you *fucking* dare.

When it comes to Grindr, you can find many, many types of people. OMG, y'all, I was about to start going through the different archetypes of gays, and it was starting to sound very *Mean Girls* cafeteria scene: "You got your freshmen, ROTC guys, preps, JV jocks, Asian nerds, cool Asians, varsity jocks, unfriendly black hotties, girls who eat their feelings," etc. Okay, sorry. Essentially, Grindr lets you select what "tribe" you consider yourself to be a part of, with options such as:

bears (hairy)

daddies (older)

gaymer (gay video gamer)

jocks (sporty)

twinks (younger and boyish)

I'm clearly a big bear daddy (read that all drawn out and in a moany voice for the full effect: biiiiig bearrrrr daaaaaddyyyyyy). Okay, I'm kidding.

The average gay may use Grindr for one of many reasons . . . or at least, there is a drop-down list of options: networking, dates, relationship, and the one nobody picks but everyone means: right now. If I had my way, the list would also include the main reasons I have the app downloaded: "looking for someone to make me guacamole," "bored and feeling insecure about my body because of everyone else's torso profile pictures," and of course "in need of someone to figure out how to use all the clickers for my damn TV because Lord knows I don't know how." *What can I say? I'm a catch!*

As someone who feels no shame in being a living, breathing sexual being, I don't believe in being coy about having the app on my phone. I think being embarrassed about having Grindr is another form of oppression we put onto ourselves, rooted in a systematically enforced belief that homosexuality is inherently wrong—while heterosexual people can discuss their OkCupid and Tinder profiles free of shame.

Sharing that shame of having the app, many users don't show their faces, as they consider themselves "discreet"—which I completely respect in terms of different people being in different places in their coming out. When they *do* have a face picture available, it can sometimes be misleading. Think of it this way: you untag any unflattering pictures on Facebook. Of all those pictures still tagged, you pick the best ones to be your profile pictures. Of those profile pictures, you pick your best one to be your Grindr picture. Sometimes, with the right lighting, the right angles, and the right photoshopping, you're a work of art . . . barely recognizable when you show up at my front door at 1:00 a.m.

On Grindr, as with OkCupid and Tinder and Scruff and Match and all those other apps, you put your best foot forward to try to find "the one." Whether that is for good or for right now, it's hundreds of thousands of people carefully constructing their profiles to make themselves as message-worthy as possible. Not to say people are never honest on these things, but you're typically not going to lead with what makes you freakiest.

Over the years of my having the app, I've had my fair share of encounters, ranging from onetime coffee dates, to substantial short-term relationships, to new friends, to business-networking opportunities, to hookups—or, as I like to call them, adult slumber parties. Some went well, some not so well, and that's the gamble when you use the app.

I should mention that with each experience I'm extremely safe, in many ways. For example, I've got a buddy system with my friend Korey, wherein we communicate when/where/who we're meeting up with, for the sake of actual physical safety. You never know who might be catfishing you. (I keep holding out that maybe it's Zac Efron catfishing me.)

One weekend in early 2013, I was invited by Taco Bell to accompany them to SXSW, an annual festival celebrating music, technology, and film. SXSW can be a lot of fun. There is so much to do, and many hot spots to check out, but in the city of Austin, Texas, during the midst of the festival, it's almost impossible to get a cab. Sure, you can always travel on the local favorite transport, a tuktuk (a cart pulled by a man on a bike). But I once saw a pretty frail guy pedaling one with calves the size of his head—it was like those douche-bag bros at the gym who forget leg day for ten years, except the exact opposite. Does that even make sense? Well, let me tell you, it was a sight and it scarred me for life, and I never felt right taking one of those tuktuks ever again. So to transport myself around Austin during SXSW, it was all about walking.

Unfortunately, the weekend prior, I drunkenly stumbled, and (although it was never confirmed by a doctor due to my lack of health care at the time) I am pretty sure I had broken my big toe. It was healing, but judging by the color of the bruise that was spreading from under my toenail to my entire toe, it was definitely not in the best condition. This was not convenient, considering all the walking.

Now, I had just finished up a full day of adventuring around Austin, and with my broken toe and the stifling heat, I was exhausted, gross, and sweaty. Not cute, and my feet were stanky. You know when you walk in your front door and take off your shoes and it's the best feeling in the world? That was me arriving back at my hotel that day.

I sat on my hotel-room bed and did what any gay would do while traveling to a new town: logged on to Grindr to see what the locals had to offer. Going to a new town is like finding a new, delicious restaurant. When you live in the same neighborhood for a year, you get used to the menu—but a new location was fresh meat. I scrolled through the assortment of gays—some locals, but mostly SXSW attendees from all over the nation. Given the mix of interests catered to by the festival, all types of gays were up for grabs: hipster music buffs, artsy-film types, and nerdy tech men . . . as well as the local varieties.

Brrrrppp! The noise of an incoming message. I checked what fate had sent my way, and a headless torso offered a simple hi. Normally, I have no interest in replying to people who don't lead with a face picture, but that day I said hi back. I checked out his profile and saw his stats: five feet six inches (around my height, preferred), interested in anything and everything, and at the bottom of his description something that I had never seen and that grabbed my attention: "into foot play."

Back in high school, I'd somehow developed a life motto of "try everything twice," with the assumption that life is too short to pass up a new opportunity, and also too short to dismiss anything just because it was shitty the first time. When it came to what *foot play* could mean, I figured, *Okay, Tyler, this is time number one, in which you try something before saying you're not into it.* Whatever foot play was, I wanted to know more. I was intrigued.

We started conversation normally, talking about what we were doing in town (he was here for work, just like me) and where we were from (both the Midwest). We exchanged more pictures. As I waited for them to load, I was bracing myself for some freaky hoof shots . . . but I received nothing but the normal Grindr exchange: face pictures in normal, everyday situations, shots of him surrounded by friends, and a picture of him shirtless at the beach. Okay, this guy isn't going to, like, chop off my feet, I guess.

Conversation continued, then finally, at just the right moment, I realized it was coming—the first mention of his main interest: toemance. It came up subtly, but I knew exactly where he was going.

"So, did you walk around a lot today for SXSW?"

"Yeah, literally everywhere."

"You could probably use a foot massage right now, no?"

It was as if I had hit the jackpot. Nothing sounded better than a foot massage, and even though I had a feeling it might go a bit further and in a kinkier direction, I was in no mood to deny the most tempting comfort of all time.

"Honestly, that sounds amazing. I'm not a local though, I have no clue where I could go." I played coy.

"Well, I mean, if you're interested, I could always give you one."

"Sure!" I replied with a faux naïveté. What could possibly go wrong? I sent him my location, and I let my friend who was staying at the same hotel as me know I was having an adult friend over for some fun, and to keep her phone near her, just in case.

"I'll be there in twenty minutes."

"Perfect! I'll take a quick shower—message when you're downstairs."

"Wait . . ."

I waited.

"Your feet are pretty smelly . . . right?"

"Yeah, I'm gross right now."

"Don't shower. I hope it's not weird, but that's really hot to me. Put on your stinkiest socks and keep your shoes on when you answer the door. I want to take them off of you."

And there it was. I was in too deep. He already knew my location. All my thoughts were rushing, and I had no clue what to do. Do I freak and tell him never mind? Do I just not reply to his message when he arrives? I was flustered and my heart was racing and I was feeling anxious and my feet stank.

So I did what anyone, I hope including you, dear reader, would do: I put on my stanky shoes.

After what felt like an hour, my phone *brrrrrp*'ed again, and my cankle connoisseur was here. I let him in the side door downstairs, and we awkwardly shook hands. He was cute, looked like his pictures, and was gentlemanly and seemed normal. I guess I didn't know what I expected? My preconceived notion of what it meant to have a foot fetish—or any fetish—was being thrown for a loop. I led him to my room, inserted my door key, and let him step in first.

Conversation followed the same lines as on Grindr, with a bit of small talk as he sat on a chair near my bed. I sat on my bed and answered his questions, but with a look of *Okay, buddy . . . let's not act like you didn't just tell me to keep my stank-nasty shoes on because you want to sniff 'em in about two minutes.* He picked up what I was laying down and said with an almost quivering voice, "So, ummmm, do you want that foot massage?"

I wasn't quite sure what to do, so I stretched and leaned back with my arms up and hands behind my head. He came closer to my feet—eyeing them as if he were Gollum and I had on the one-(toe)ring-to-rule-them-all. He took my Adidas tennies in his hands, and although he said nothing, his eyes moaned, *My precioussssssssss.*

Now, I won't lie and say that when he started deeply inhaling the scent of my shoes, I didn't cringe inwardly. Listen, I'm new to this, I wasn't expecting to have my feet worshipped on a Thursday night. He slowly unlaced each shoe, holding these beaten-down shoes with as much care as one would give to a glass slipper. Then, one at a time, in a reverse Cinderella's prince maneuver, he revealed what were to be his prized possessions . . . my rancid feet.

Now, I don't want to alarm anyone reading this book, but there is *always something fundamentally wrong with each and every person you could potentially date.* Nobody is perfect! What's wrong with me? you ask. Well, ask any of my friends, and they'll tell you that after I've been wearing shoes all day, my feet stink like something unholy. *It's not like I don't try to fix this though!* I often preemptively sneak into the bathroom upon arriving anywhere and wash my feet in the bathtub or sink. I get it, nobody wants to smell my feet, and I fix the problem before anyone sniffs and looks around. *I am the first to acknowledge my gross-smelling feet, and I am sorry.*

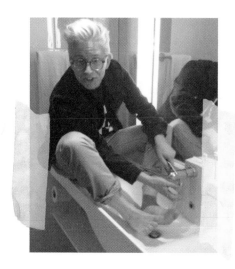

But *this guy* . . . not only did he not mind . . . this guy lived for it. His entire life had been leading up to this moment, and with each deep inhalation, homeboy found new life. It was as if every breath prior to now were second-grade oxygen. The look on his face communicated it all: if my feet had a sound, my toes were his jam. If he was in pain, only my feet could heal him. If he was looking for perfection, only I could nail it. If he was giving my toes a score, he'd count each foot as a perfect ten. *Enough foot puns, he was living for my feet.*

But it wasn't just him that was living . . . I was living too. His massage was tender, sensual, generous—and I was in heaven.

Sniffing led to a whole lot more, and although I'd never fantasized about this before, I think I found a new calling. I won't go any further about what happened next, but I became so open-minded during that slumber party that I (after he pleaded for it) even stepped on his cheek a little? Who knew that I, Tyler Oakley, would tap-dance on someone's face for their pleasure? God, I'm such a giver. A modern-day Mother Toeresa. (I can't stop, please forgive me.)

Things wrapped up as they usually do. He went to the bathroom, and I lay there on my bed silently pondering everything that had just happened. The door opened and he reappeared, all smiles. "You seemed to be into that."

My first instinct was to make an excuse or to get bashful or to change the subject . . . but then I realized I was in good company. I could be honest, and this guy was the one who seemed to be holding back. "Actually, yeah, that was kind of amazing."

Maybe we all go through life carefully constructing our profiles to say what we're looking for, all while not saying anything that might scare people away . . . and after a time we start to believe what we're putting out there. Our fear of people's rejecting the things that make us happy limits how much happiness we can actually find. I guess when we're a bit more honest with ourselves and others, we might get more of what we actually desire. Now, any nice gentleman out there want me to step on their face?

unhappiest birthday

OR THE FIRST TWENTY-FOUR YEARS OF MY LIFE,
the "Happy Birthday" song was tolerable. On my
twenty-fifth birthday, it gave me a full-blown anxiety
attack.

I was used to celebrating my birthday at YouTube conventions. I had done so for the past few years, but this year's
conventionwas different. It was the first time I'd attended
since reaching 1 million subscribers. Though I didn't feel any
different personally, my experience at the convention changed
dramatically.

YouTube conventions had always been pleasant. They're
a chance for excited viewers to come together at a convention
center with the hopes of learning about the industry, meeting
Internet friends, and sometimes catching a glimpse of their favorite YouTube creators. The attendance numbers get higher
and higher every year, and now tens of thousands of teens arrive, hoping for a selfie with one of the hundreds of featured
YouTubers.

I've been attending conventions since I had one thousand subscribers, back when conventions were called "gatherings." My first was in Toronto in 2008, and maybe sixty people showed up. I've since gone to every Playlist Live (Florida), and almost every VidCon (Los Angeles), with some appearances at other conventions such as Summer in the City (London), VloggerFair (Seattle), ITAtube (Italy), and FanFest (Singapore and Australia). My worst experience at a convention happened in 2014. I was going through a weird time with some of my friends, with myself, and with my content—I was trying to figure out who and what I was as a person and as a YouTuber.

It was the day before my twenty-fifth birthday, and I had already spent my entire day doing meet and greets, surprise merchandise signings, panels, and interviews. By the end of the day, I was exhausted. A small group of close YouTube friends joined me for my birthday dinner. We hired van-size cabs to take care of us for the evening. They would whisk us away from the convention hotel to make sure we had both privacy and downtime from the hustle of the weekend. After dinner, our vans picked us up and headed back toward our hotel. As our driver pulled into the hotel's parking lot, we tried our best to explain the uniqueness of the fan situation and recommend the best route to avoid any commotion. My usual convention tactic to avoid causing a scene during personal downtime is a head-down, sunglasses, undetected flyby. It's not that I don't want to interact with viewers—it's that I try to be very deliberate about when I'm working and when I need to relax—for my own sanity and health. Unfortunately, an extralong panel van isn't necessarily easy to sneak past a throng of hyperaware superfans. We were spotted instantly.

The chaos that ensued was terrifying for everyone. A mob of teenagers swarmed the van, and the driver began to panic. Against our desperate pleas to maintain our speed, he slowed to a halt, scared he might run over someone. Within seconds we were completely surrounded, and I felt my stomach drop. Thirty screaming fans, adorned in YouTuber merchandise and flower crowns, slapped their hands against the windows of the van on all sides, shouting at the top of their lungs. They pressed their faces against the tinted windows, and we jumped toward the center of the van, as if being attacked by zombies. As each of us were identified through the tinted windows and announced to the restless natives outside, the rhythmic pounding crescendoed.

When they spotted me, they burst into singing "Happy Birthday." My head spun. Our horror movie of a situation was now a . . . zombie musical? In which the undead serenade us before devouring our brains? Somehow, the effect was less silly than creepy, and to this day I still hear it in my head in a haunting minor chord. My heart raced, and my body went weak. I wanted more than anything else to jump across the seats and stomp the driver's foot down on the pedal—instead, I sat paralyzed, terrified, and trapped.

I never meant to snap, but when you're pushed into a corner, it's fight or flight. Without thinking, I slammed my fists against the window as hard as I could and began screaming at the mob. *"Do you think this is fucking safe?"*

The singing stopped immediately. Fans backed up slowly, as if *I* were the deranged one.

I kept screaming the same thing over and over: *"Do you honestly think this is safe?"*

My YouTube friends sat in silence, gawking at me. With a wide enough berth to start moving the van, our driver slowly accelerated forward.

I slumped into my seat, heart racing, embarrassed that I had let myself be pushed to the edge. I just wanted to get back to my hotel room.

The second I stepped into my room, I broke down. Conventions had always been fun before, but that was when I felt that I had control and could handle what I was signing up for. I lay on my hotel bed in silence. I felt betrayed. I had voluntarily surrendered my birthday weekend for this. I felt like a selfie prop or a collectible souvenir, not a human. Yes, I was crying and obviously being dramatic, but my emotions were rooted in something deeper than this isolated event. In my pursuit of success, was I trading away too much of my humanity? Had I lost all control? Was I even enjoying what I was doing? Was *I* the deranged one?

I thought about what my life would be like if I just deleted my social media accounts that night. Would I be able to move on from my life online? I had spent the past seven years making videos and sharing every detail of my life. What would happen if I just stopped? Time would march forward. Viewers would continue to watch YouTube. Conventions would still buzz with excitement.

While I was feeling more alone and lost than ever before,

my phone vibrated next to my head. I reached up and saw a text from my friend Mamrie Hart. Mamrie is an absolute legend of YouTube. She has a show called *You Deserve a Drink*, and she's one of the funniest people I've ever met. Once we went to a zombie-apocalypse maze in Las Vegas where we had to fight off actors playing the undead with paintball guns. Heartfelt and usually a bit tipsy, she's like your hilarious aunt who spends most of her time adding puns to her dog's Instagram. *You coming to the party?* she asked.

That night, like every night at YouTube conventions, there was a party for guests to attend and mingle. Over the years, my schedules at conventions got busier and more chaotic, which made the events more exhausting to attend. While I used to go to every party, I now found bliss in the comfort of my own hotel bed with a few close friends and some red wine. But this night, I wondered if maybe the distraction of a YouTube party was what I needed. *Sure,* I replied.

I made my way down in the elevator and texted one of my best friends, Hannah Hart, to let her know I was en route to the party. Hannah was an accidental YouTuber who went viral with her first video and absolutely ran with it. Since then, she's starred in movies, had a *New York Times* Best Seller, and fostered one of the most inspiring communities online. She gets drunk and cooks, with a show called *My Drunk Kitchen*. Besides all that, she's hilarious and warm and knows when I need a hug, and just how long the hug needs to be for me to not feel like crying anymore. She replied to let me know she'd just arrived to the party and that I should let her know when I got there.

The only way to get to the party was by riding in the back-seat of a golf cart from the hotel to the event center. During the ride over, I tried to calm myself down. I thought about how much I wanted a glass of red wine to help me take the edge off. I entered the front door of the party and was bombarded with thumping bass. The party was packed. I knew a handful of guests, but all I wanted was to find my friends.

In previous years, I was typically the YouTuber who plucked up his courage and went up to the top creators to ask for a selfie. As I attempted to squeeze through the crowds of people, I started to feel that maybe I had finally become one of those top creators. Every few steps, I was being tugged by people asking for a picture. I wasn't used to this, and considering the day's earlier circumstances, I wasn't prepared for it. Normally, I'd be happy to oblige, but after the incident in the van, taking selfies with people I didn't know was the last thing I wanted to do. Unfortunately, I'm a people pleaser, and I gritted my teeth through each shot. I increased my pace, weaving in and out of the crowd. I pulled out my phone to try to get ahold of any of my actual friends, but I had no service. It was 11:50 p.m. Ten minutes until my birthday, and I couldn't find anyone. I stepped a few paces farther, and I was stopped by some acquaintances. They warned me not to go too far away, 'birthday boy, because it's almost time." *Oh, God, are all of these strangers planning something?*

I became frantic trying to find my friends. I ran into some creators I knew vaguely, and they saw I was noticeably distressed. "Here, take a shot, it'll calm you down," they suggested. I took the shot glass in my hand and thought it over. If I took it,

I'd relax, but was this the only way? In an instant, I considered my mom's mom, a heavy drinker for as long as I'd known her. I remembered her hugging me when I was younger, and I could smell the reek of stale beer. At that moment, a pair of hands landed on my shoulders behind me. I spun, startled, and found Hannah grinning. I set the shot glass down and hugged her.

"Five minutes!" she yelled over the thumping beat.

I leaned into her ear. "I need out of here."

She pulled back and saw that the seriousness on my face matched the tone of my voice. She took my hand and led me through the crowd. We burst through the front doors of the party and into the fresh air. I was instantly relieved from all sense of suffocation. She hailed us a golf cart, and we made our way back to the hotel. I leaned my head back and closed my eyes as the breeze cooled me down.

Hannah put her arm around me and squeezed my shoulder. "Happy birthday . . ."

Eyes still closed, I smiled. This was the definition of quality over quantity.

We got back to our hotel, changed into sweatpants, and hung out in my room. A few other friends joined us, including Mamrie, who informed me that the party's DJ was planning on announcing my birthday, with shots readied for everyone and a birthday sing-along. I cackled at the thought—how suddenly would their expressions have dropped had I succumbed to a full-blown panic attack and had to be carried out of my own celebration?

That night, when pushed to an edge I had never before encountered, I was offered the chance to binge, to escape through alcohol as I felt my mom's mom did: an easy escape, but one that could have had a ripple effect on how I'd handle my lowest lows in the future. Luckily, I said yes—not to alcohol, or to the attention of hundreds of strangers at a party, but to the company of people I cared about, who let me lean on them during one of my most vulnerable moments.

melancholy fantasies

IF YOU EVER FIND YOURSELF MORE OFTEN HOPING that the flights you're on crash instead of landing safely, you're probably not in a good place. For a good part of 2014, that's where I was. It was the most professionally successful year of my life so far, but I completely lost myself personally. Think the lyrics of Britney Spears's chart-topping song "Lucky": *And the world is spinning, and she keeps on winning / but tell me, what happens when it stops?*

The larger my platform, the more scrutiny I faced. I realized that the more influence one has, the higher the expectations, and because of this I began to doubt every move I'd make and every word I'd say, for fear of being misinterpreted and labeled as evil for the rest of time. Instead of letting that paralyze me, I figured that regardless of how anyone felt about Tyler Oakley as a person, if I were to fight tooth and nail to create the most productive year of my life, nobody would be able to deny my work ethic. And I was absolutely right. Between my producing ninety-two videos, creating my podcast, going on the Slumber

Party Tour, attending almost every convention, and working almost every award show's red carpet, @tyleroakley was slaying the game.

But, in the words of our good friend Britney Spears, if there's nothing missing in my life, then why do these tears come at night? Well, for me, it was because while all of those successes were happening, I slowly began to forget who Tyler Oakley was. I could always introduce @tyleroakley in a meeting or at a party, but when asked anything about the man behind the username, my answers began to fade from my own vision.

What were my hobbies? Well, I spent most of my time working. What were my passions? Well, my job, mostly. What did I do for fun? My job was fun! Those were the things I'd tell myself, my first dates, and my mom when I went home for the holidays. I think most people saw through it, but I didn't. I believed every word. One of those "fake it till you make it" situations. And it's not to say that my hobbies, passions, and what I find fun don't include my job—but if that's all you have, what happens when you need a break? I didn't know how to take a break. I had no clue how to turn off or stop.

When I went home for the holidays, I was ready to shower my mom with expensive gifts after such a successful year. My family has never had it all (or most, or more than some), and being able to help in some way makes me feel that I'm contributing, even if I live on the other side of the country. When I asked my mom what she wanted for Christmas, she could have said anything and gotten it from me.

Instead, she sat for a moment, looked me in the eye, and

told me not to be upset about what she was about to request. "Honestly, I just want it to feel like you're *home* while you're here. Your dad is getting older, I'm getting older, the kids are growing up, and before you know it, you're going to look back and not remember any of it."

It was true. I don't visit Michigan much, and when I am home, I'm buried in my phone, in my computer, on a call, in a meeting, writing, working, editing. All she wanted was for me to stop for a second, relax, and share a moment with my family. The closest I get to a moment of relaxation is typically on a flight—and only then when the food cart comes around and I don't have space on my tray table for both my dinner and my laptop. Sorry, laptop, even airplane food will always trump you.

During those moments on flights, sitting peacefully with my earbuds in (so the people next to me won't talk to me regardless of whether I'm actually listening to anything), I'd begin my newfound activity as the newest member of the mile-high morbidity club.

If the wing flies off the plane, I won't have to attend that red carpet, I thought to myself, midair and midsip of red wine. *I'll never have to take another meeting,* I considered, imagining a fatal slip of the pilot's hand, midlanding. I wasn't suicidal. I hadn't actually considered killing myself in many years (since the first love of my life)—no, this melancholy was a lot less intense and urgent. This was me imagining a break from it all, coupled with the sad realization that the only way I could possibly imagine a break was through a devastating act of God.

Not to say that I wasn't living my dream life, because I totally was. But my dream life was a collection of addicting things. I've never gotten into heavy drugs, mainly because the family business is substance-abuse therapy, and my parents would be so annoyed if I was found dead with heroin up my nose, or however one does it. So I get my kicks elsewhere. But when you're addicted to achievement, in a profession that doesn't allow vacations, off-seasons, or even the idea that your field should be considered work in the first place, it's hard to put down the success pipe. So I found myself picking it up, over and over, with conventions to attend, flights to board, videos to film, goals to beat, and numbers to reach. Numbers became my drug of choice. But numbers are infinite, and no milestone or threshold can exhaust them.

When I was younger, I played a video game online creating characters and leveling them up. The higher the level you reached, the longer it took you to get to the next level. It was a hamster wheel, and for years I paid $9.95 a month to be a part of it. I was addicted. I became so addicted that my parents began to limit my access to it, and they went to great lengths to control my usage.

When they weren't home, they'd disconnect the Internet by unhooking and hiding the connector between the cable and the modem. So obviously, middle school me rollerbladed to the nearest hardware store to find my own replacement, one that I could hook up while they were gone. I'd play my game in complete silence, and when I heard their car turn into the driveway, my stalwart guards (the family dogs) would begin to whine in anticipation. This was my cue to sprint to my parents' room, unhook my Internet connector, and leave everything exactly how they had left it, all before they came in through the front door. This became my daily ritual, and from the moment I got home from school to the moment my parents were home, I'd be playing. At night, they'd take my keyboard away when they went to bed so that I wouldn't be wasting away in front of a screen. But when everyone was asleep, I'd wake up in the middle of the night, pull out my own keyboard that I had bought with the birthday money I'd saved up, and I'd play until my parents woke up to go to work. I thought about my game all day, every day. I wanted to be the best character, I wanted to have the best items, I wanted to reach the highest numbers. No, higher than the highest.

To get my video game fix, I even committed minor identity theft and credit-card fraud. The $9.95-a-month fee may not seem like much, but it was tough for a middle schooler. I stole my stepbrother's mom's credit card. When she found out, she told my parents, and they realized that I had a legitimate problem. But how was I to keep up my progress if I couldn't pay for the subscription? Did nobody understand my predicament? Clearly not. I was forced to write her a letter of apology, with a check for $9.95 enclosed. Ugh.

These days, more than a decade later, my addictive personality lives on, and my game of choice is still online. The major difference is, now, @tyleroakley is my character. The level-ups come from real-life hustle—collaborating, attending events, working on projects, and always, always chasing the numbers.

When I would imagine my flight crashing, it was never because I hated my life. I loved my life. It was always because it would just be so much easier. Easier than following through on the obligations I had made, putting on a suit and making a good impression at an important meeting, or networking at an event. I began to enjoy fewer of my experiences. Instead, I would instantly catalog those opportunities as things I had accomplished, and it was now on to the next thing. I used to joke about various accomplishments being desirable solely because they'd make good entries for my *Wikipedia* entry, but then, in the back of my mind, that joke became kind of true. A hint of truth is behind every joke, increasingly so if the joke becomes your mantra.

Or maybe the plane would be taken down by a terrorist. I'd be sitting in my seat, unimpressed by the crazy man screaming, *"Nobody move!"* Like, honestly, dude, don't worry, I won't be lifting a finger. In the hubbub of the takeover, I'd slowly recline my seat, wondering what my last tweet was before we took off. I'd hope it wasn't something dumb. Last tweets are the new "famous last words." If God is listening, I request that He not take me while any of these linger as my last earthly tweet:

RT my last tweet for a DM!

@zacefron pls follow me.

heart-eyes emoji butts *heart-eyes emoji*

Nebraska, I am in you.

Slay me, Queen @lindsaylohan.

I often used to joke with Korey about creating videos to be uploaded upon my death. I always thought it would be so nice to have the final word and the last laugh. I don't think I'd use this opportunity to tell anyone off who had wronged me while I was living, just more to have an end cap to the plot of my YouTube channel. I guess, even when considering death, I'm looking for good marketing opportunities. Perhaps a recommendation for a how-to audiobook on grieving. Morbid, but possibly lucrative. This too was a joke that I later began to consider legitimately.

It should also be noted that I'd never actively work to take down my flight. My blah attitude was not looking to kill off an entire cabin of passengers in exchange for a break in my work schedule. I'm just saying that for a time in 2014, I probably shouldn't have been given the responsibilities of an exit-row seat.

Realizing all of this, and acknowledging that I daydreamed about turbulence shifting the luggage above me so vigorously that a carry-on would fall out and break my neck, inspired me to reflect on my religious upbringing back in mid-Michigan.

When I was in my single digits, I was subjected to the worst torture you can possibly inflict on a child: Catholic mass. For those who have never attended, it's an hour of monotonous ritual and tradition. Between singing noncatchy hymns, eating stale crackers that represent the body of Christ, and shaking hands unsanitarily with dozens of strangers while mumbling, "Peace be with you," it was, ironically, my own definition of hell.

I'd spend most of my time during mass imagining all the ways I could die just to get out of enduring it. Perhaps a statue of an apostle or even Mary could fall and impale me. Maybe a Jesus statue's crown of thorns could poke me right in a pressure point, while I was heading to the confessional. Maybe a rosary could get snagged around my neck, hanging me. Maybe while I was lighting a candle, the flames would catch on my pleated khakis and spread too quickly for me to be saved. Or maybe someone could give me Ebola via a peace-be-with-you handshake. When given the chance to lead my family into the pews, I'd always opt to sit under pendulous light fixtures and especially next to any stained glass, just in case an earthquake hit. *Michigan is overdue for a huge earthquake*, I thought to myself, *and if it's going to hit, a huge glass shard had better sever my head*, please *and* thank you. *Err, I mean, amen. There we go.*

Perhaps someone would accidentally spill poison into the holy water, and one flick onto my skin would fell me. Or maybe actual holy water would touch my sinful closeted-homosexual skin, and I'd melt like the wicked witch in *The Wizard of Oz*. Snapping back to reality, nine-year-old me would look down at my ill-fitting black dress shoes and think of how disappointingly they compared to ruby slippers. Then I'd look back up and remember that none of my fantasies could possibly happen, and that I'd have to live through mass until I could finally return to my house and unwind from the stress of organized religion. There's no place like home, after all.

Sitting in mass felt like the most alone I could ever feel. I was surrounded by people who didn't get me, who I didn't trust and couldn't reach out to, and if I had to sit through one more second if it, I might just burst. Sometimes, in 2014, that's how meetings felt. Or red carpets. Which made me feel so guilty, because these are things that are making my wildest dreams come true, and they're things so many people would kill to have. But if I've learned one thing about feelings, it's that sometimes they're *happening*, regardless of how good you have it or how bad anyone else has it or any other kind of sense you might try to make.

A lot of my 2014 was spent working myself into a fury, and having nobody to talk to when I reached my lowest points. Growing up, I was sent to therapist after therapist (eating-disorder stuff, divorce stuff), and I would sit silent for the entire hour on the couch. The therapist would ask questions, and I'd stare off into space, hoping by some miracle death would come swooping in on leathery wings. Maybe a girl in the next room was possessed by demons and would have a bad sense of depth perception, and the telekinetic terror she meant to cause in her own therapist's office would be misdirected and accidentally hit my room, causing the shelf of psychology books to crash down on me in a heap and smother me to death. That was a lot more plausible than my actually opening my mouth and telling the therapist what was wrong, and my parents held out hope enough for *that* to keep hauling me to the sessions.

Maybe I have these thoughts while I'm a mile above the earth because that's where I feel most disconnected. I always say, "If you're going through a difficult time, reaching out is one of the bravest things you can possibly do," but what if you're stuck in a jet, hurtling through the sky, with no access to Wi-Fi or iMessage? I mean, I never hope that my cab turns into oncoming traffic, or that my train combusts spontaneously. No, any other mode of transportation allows me to easily pick up my phone and call the people who matter, the people who get me, the people who care.

When it's 2:00 a.m. and I'm feeling lonely or discouraged

at home, with no friends or family to call due to time zones, I usually start replying to you guys on Twitter. Y'all are all over the world, and at any moment of the day, someone is always in my replies saying something nice, when I need it most. There are always people to reach out to online.

Maybe that's why after a Wi-Fi–less flight full of fantasies of my in-flight dining being laced with arsenic, I come to my senses as soon as I land. A habit I've picked up over the years of tweeting my landing with *(Insert city or state name here), I am in you* has become less of an announcement of my arrival and more of a plea for interaction, connection, and restarting the conversation with people who make me feel less alone. When I see y'all responding to my *I am in you* tweet, both sides feel connected—y'all know I'm there, reading your replies, and ready to respond. I acknowledge you, I notice you, and I see you.

I'm happy to report that I'm writing this chapter in 2015 on a flight, on my way back to California. In a few short hours, I'll be tweeting, *Los Angeles, I am in you.* I can't wait to see the replies. I'm in a better place now, and I spent exactly none of my flight hoping that when I flushed the plane's toilet, the suction would be too much and my internal organs would all be vacuumed out, leaving me a lifeless husk in a locked airplane lavatory. Instead, I've spent my flight daydreaming about how I can't wait to walk through the front door of my own home, where I plan not to work myself to death, but instead to work myself back to life. As grateful as I am for the opportunities, I never again want to board a plane that I wish explodes mid-flight, only to land and make my way to an obligation that I hope is directly below a heavy, poorly installed chandelier. I want to take only the opportunities that make me feel alive. I want to meet people who want to meet Mathew Tyler Oakley, not @tyleroakley. When I do meet them, I want to have plenty to tell them about what makes me happy while I'm not on the Internet.

epilogue

Okay, people, we're now coming to the end of our *Binge*. I hope I haven't given you so much of what you thought you wanted that now you've reached a state of disgust, but just enough so that you feel sated, self-indulgent, and maybe a little naughty.

My fondest wish is that I've demonstrated by my flawed but earnest example the value of taking chances, pushing beyond our comfort levels, dusting ourselves off after our inevitable humiliations, and remaining open to the life and feelings and possibilities that are happening while we're busy either chasing phantoms of success or trying to outrun our fears. I don't know that I've conquered my Big Bad Wolf, but I have learned to walk beside him and tame him some with the humility and values shared by my family, cherished friends, and loved ones. I've also found a few experiences that are definitely worth binging on, and I hope you have, too.

In the spirit of walking alongside our demons, please enjoy the elementary school picture to the left. The takeaway? When life gives you lice, find a plastic bag, rock your look, and enjoy a cheeseburger like a boss.

If there's one thing worth binging on, it's making it work.

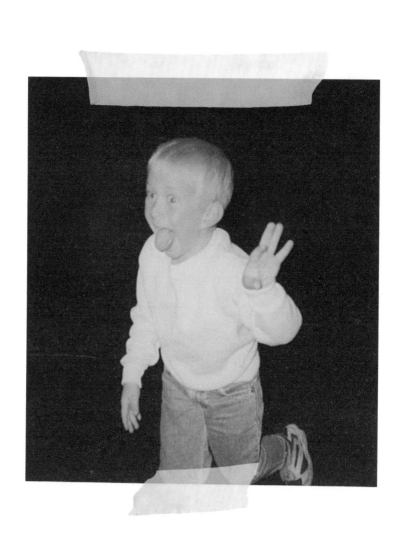

acknowledgments

To my book people, thank you for believing in me. To my brilliant editor, Jeremie Ruby-Strauss, I'm honored that you were a part of this project. Before we began, you showed up to my Slumber Party Tour in a onesie and I knew you would be perfect; emails from you were the highlight of my day. Thank you to my literary agent, Cait Hoyt, for your unparalleled patience and for believing in this book before anyone else, including me. Thank you, Nina Cordes, Ygraine Cadlock, Jen Bergstrom, Louise Burke, Carolyn Reidy, Iain Macgregor, Liz Psaltis, Jennifer Robinson, Steph Deluca, Susan Rella, John Vairo, Lisa Litwack, and everyone at Simon & Schuster and Gallery Books. I couldn't have had a better crew for this book.

To my team, thank you for helping me navigate this weird life I'm lucky enough to live. Thank you, Lisa, for helping me literally achieve my dreams and for telling me I "look so thin lately" when you know I feel frumpy. Thank you, Korey, for keeping me sane and for being my best friend and for making me laugh and for giving me hugs when you can tell I need them. To Mia, Steve, Rachel, Cassandra, Jordan, Max, Gabe, Emma, Tim, Mike, Simone, Vinny, Brent, Meghan, Ashley, Amy, Laura, Ronan, each of you plays such an important role in the success of My People Entertainment, Inc. Thank you.

To my family, thank you for not always understanding me or my path but supporting unwaveringly. Moms and dads, sorry for what you've read, but honestly you're to blame for all of this mess that is me. Siblings, thank you for loving me despite how bad I am at returning texts when I'm not home, and for making me put my phone away when I am. You all make Michigan magical for me. Nieces and nephews, don't read this book yet.

To my friends, thank you for being the shoulders I'm able to lean on when all of this starts to be a little too much. To my YouTube friends, thank you for being coworkers in a career that is overwhelmingly solitary. You inspire me and support me and I'm so very grateful to have #TeamInternet in my life. To my non-Internet friends, thank you for putting up with me since day one, whether you're my 20s from Okemos, my MSU ResLife buddies, or my SF gays, I appreciate you.

And finally, to my people, none of this would be possible without you. That is no exaggeration. You make fun of my Twitter layout and call me dad and watch my videos and listen to my podcasts and come to my tour and you bought this book. You are protective of me, and always tweet me telling me to take care of myself. I hope we meet someday so I can thank you for all of this in person. If you're reading this, tweet me (@tyleroakley) a selfie of you and the book, with the hashtag #BingeBook. I'm sending love to people who do.

photo credits

Courtesy of Jacquelyn Fields: pgs. 2, 6, 20, 28, 31, 34, 40, 46, 48, 61, 65, 68, 73, 77, 79, 80, 86, 159, 167, 186, 211, 212, 214, 218–221, 302, 304

Courtesy of the author: pgs. 14, 43, 75, 104, 107, 127, 129, 215, 234, 242, 262,

Courtesy of Korey Kuhl: pgs. 216, 258

Courtesy of Lisa Filipelli: pg. 281

Courtesy of the White House Photo Office: pg. 252

Courtesy of Alex Goldschmidt: pg. 240

Courtesy of Robert Andrew Perez: pg. 195